# the foodie teen

## alessandra peters

# the foodie teen

## alessandra peters

Over 100 nutritious and wholesome recipes from a teenage blogging sensation

MICHAEL JOSEPH
*an imprint of*
PENGUIN BOOKS

# DEDICATION

To my family, without whose constant support and taste-testing this dream would never have become a reality, and to all those who have supported and encouraged me along the way – it truly means the world.

MICHAEL JOSEPH

UK | USA | Canada | Ireland | Australia
India | New Zealand | South Africa

Michael Joseph is part of the Penguin Random House group of companies whose addresses can be found at global.penguinrandomhouse.com.

First published 2016
001

Text and images copyright © Alessandra Peters, 2016
Additional photography © Issy Croker, 2016
Design by nicandlou, 2016

Printed in China

A CIP catalogue record for this book is available from the British Library

HARDBACK ISBN: 978–0–718–18251–9
TRADE PAPERBACK ISBN: 978–0–718–18347–9

www.greenpenguin.co.uk

MIX
Paper from
responsible sources
FSC® C018179

Penguin Random House is committed to a sustainable future for our business, our readers and our planet. This book is made from Forest Stewardship Council® certified paper.

# CONTENTS

# INTRODUCTION

I've always absolutely adored food. When I was little, I spent hours in the bustling kitchen, mesmerized by the wonderful smells, brilliant sounds and incredible flavours springing from the pots and pans lining the cooker. The first thing I ever made was a completely lopsided, slightly overcooked banana cake that I'd accidentally loaded with way too much salt (*note to self:* teaspoons are not the same thing as tablespoons!). I was so happy to have actually cooked something semi-edible all by myself that this set off a life-long love of cooking.

When I first had to start eating a healthy diet and changing my lifestyle after I was diagnosed with an autoimmune disease and lots of food intolerances, I remember instantly thinking that I was condemned to a life of bland, boring and tasteless food. Luckily, I was totally wrong!

As I started to cook with more nutritious foods, I not only began to feel so much better, with boundless energy and clearer skin, but also discovered how absolutely delicious fresh, healthy cooking can be. In a few months, I had gone from constant exhaustion to feeling truly fantastic. Eating well had transformed my life, so I started a blog (which I not-so-creatively called 'The Foodie Teen'!), and to my shock and surprise my recipes started reaching people all over the world. I'm so excited to have the opportunity to be able to share this book with you in the hope that it might help you lead a healthier life, whether you cook every single recipe or just gain a little inspiration and hopefully a few new favourites.

I'm especially happy to be able to help other teenagers and young people – I know it can often seem patronizing and downright boring when you're constantly being told what you can and can't eat by adults, who don't seem to understand that it's really hard to eat well while you're juggling school, work, a social life and a million other things, so I hope that, as a teenager myself who's in the same situation, I can share my tips in a more helpful way. From breakfasts worth getting out of bed for, to information about prepping and planning in advance to make sure you're never without a nutritious snack, there are all sorts of tips to help you take responsibility for your own health. I'm just an average seventeen-year-old, so if I can do it, anyone can!

I personally don't eat grains, dairy or legumes because of my autoimmune disease, food intolerances and other health issues and I feel a lot better without them, but just because it works for me doesn't mean that it'll work for you too. Our bodies are very complicated things and there isn't one way of eating which is best for us all. I think it's important to experiment and see what works for you. I can't eat dairy products, for example, but for many people, organic dairy is part of a well-rounded diet as well as a great source of healthy fats and calcium. I've included some suggestions where you might want to use dairy instead. However, I think we can all agree that everyone benefits from eating a more varied, nutritious diet, so I hope my recipes give you some inspiration to try different dishes and ingredients you haven't come across before.

The recipes range from red pepper chicken fajitas with tomato salsa and a coriander-spiked guacamole to incredibly gooey and decadent salted caramel brownies, so don't worry about missing out on anything! There's also lots of information about stocking your cupboards, making the basics and sourcing ingredients.

As well as all the food (there's a lot of it!), there are some helpful guides to the various parts of living a healthy lifestyle, from reducing your stress levels and developing a more positive body image, to making your own natural beauty

products without any unpronounceable chemicals in order to nourish your skin and reduce inflammation, because being healthier involves all parts of your life, from the food you eat to what you put on your skin.

Rather than telling you to follow yet another unsustainable and unrealistic diet, I want to encourage you just to focus on enjoying wholesome, unprocessed, nutritious meals. This simple, natural way of eating isn't a fad – it's a lifestyle change which will help you to take charge of your health and discover a better, more energetic and healthier version of yourself (bonus: you get to eat brownies and ice cream too!). I think it's really important to move far away from 'diet' culture and all the faddy, restrictive and frankly ridiculous information we're blasted with by the media, especially as teenagers.

What with the 'celeb diets' we see in magazines, society's obsession with counting and tracking everything we put into our mouths, and 'healthy' meal plans posted all over the internet promoting restrictive eating, it can be really difficult to listen to our bodies and value nutrition over numbers. Hopefully, the recipes and information in this book will help you do just that, along with developing your interest in cooking and proving just how delicious and simple a healthy lifestyle can be.

Let's get cooking!

*alessandra*
*x*

# MY UNPROCESSED, REAL FOOD AND HEALTHFUL LIVING PHILOSOPHY

Living a healthier life really is a lot simpler than you may think. Base your meals around seasonal vegetables and roots with some sustainable, high-welfare protein sources on the side, seasoned and spiced up with plenty of fresh herbs and exciting spices. You can enjoy a handful of protein-rich roasted nuts, a piece of fruit, or the occasional homemade treat as a snack. Stick to things that don't come out of a box or package as much as you can, and embrace whole, real, unprocessed foods for the healthiest approach.

I try to avoid processed foods, refined stuff, chemical preservatives, food colourings, artificial or refined sugars and hydrogenated oils as much as possible. I know that probably sounds quite overwhelming, but consider that some of these foods may cause spikes in blood sugar, inflammation in your body and have often been so processed that by the time they reach your plate it's hard for your body to even recognize them! Instead of eating highly-processed packaged foods, turn to fresh, healthful options full of vitamins, minerals and fibre.

It's also best to try to buy organic foods as often as you can. I also prefer avoiding anything containing or raised on genetically modified organisms (GMOs), although they're not permitted in all countries. These foods have been artificially altered using biotechnology in order to mostly withstand powerful herbicides or produce their own pesticides, and at the moment it is unclear whether they are of any benefit to the diet. In order to avoid GMOs and pesticides, it's best to try and buy organic foods as often as you can. Organic farming protects the environment and limits the use of artificial fertilizers, synthetic pesticides, growth regulators and hormones. It's the best choice for your health if you can source and afford it. As a general rule of thumb, you should try to stick with organic produce if the fruit or vegetable has a thin skin or if you're going to eat the skin (this includes apples, pears, peaches, berries, leafy greens, cucumbers, tomatoes and peppers), while thicker-skinned fruit and vegetables such as bananas, avocados, pineapples and mangoes generally have less pesticide residue and are OK to buy conventionally.

Of course, nobody is able to eat perfectly one hundred per cent of the time, and being overly strict or obsessive about always sourcing the 'perfect' ingredients can certainly lead to an unhealthy mindset! When it comes to ingredients, just try to do the best you can in the situation you're in, whatever that may be. Many of us are in a position where buying everything organic just isn't viable, so don't stress about it if that's the case.

Remember to indulge in a treat every so often, and if you do eat something that might not have been the best choice, focus on eating well at your next meal rather than beating yourself up about what's happened in the past. It's important to keep a balance – being too controlling about your diet is definitely not a good thing, so make sure to have some fun and enjoy a cookie or two.

## BUT WHAT ABOUT CALORIES?

Calories are not created equal, which is just one of the many reasons why it's so important to get used to focusing on what's actually in what you're eating rather than on how many calories' worth of it you're having. For example, we all know that 200 calories' worth of a Snickers bar is a lot worse for you than 200 calories' worth of a salad. Yes, it's the same number of calories and yes, both of those foods contain exactly 837 i.c of energy, but I'm sure you can imagine that they're going to have a very different effect on how your body functions, your energy levels and your mood.

One of the most important things to consider is that the calories in a food source do not dictate how satisfied or energetic you'll feel after consuming it. It's easy to eat 500 calories of cake, but can you imagine eating 5 apples (that's the same amount of calories) in one go? High-quality calories found in nutrient-rich seasonal fruits will fill you up and keep you satiated for much longer. If you eat calories from poor-quality foods with refined sugars and processed grains like a slice of cake, they throw off your appetite-regulating hormones and lead to you being hungry again soon after you've finished eating – I'm sure you've experienced being hungry just an hour or two after eating a huge plate of fast food!

What I'm trying to say is that the quality of what you're eating is much more important than the quantity of calories. When you eat a healthful diet of nutritious foods which keep you full and also contain lots of beneficial vitamins and minerals, there is absolutely no need to be obsessive about calories. Focus on having a balance of nutrients, listening to your body, eating when you're hungry and eating mindfully (that is, chew your food properly and take time to sit down and eat it!) instead. Be sure to concentrate on nutrition over numbers: the calorific value of a food won't tell you how you'll feel after eating it, how satisfied you'll be or whether it's a good choice for your health – it's just a number!

## GOOD FAT, BAD FAT

Moving on to another dietary demon: fat. Fats are not all bad for you. In fact, they're vital to your health and wellbeing! Over the last few decades, as food producers have replaced many full-fat things with lower fat alternatives, levels of diabetes and obesity have sky-rocketed. This is because instead of unprocessed, full-fat items, everyone has been encouraged to stick to highly processed, 'low-fat' products. The problem with these so-called 'healthier' reduced-fat options is that they are highly processed and often have sugar added to maintain flavour; they can lead to weight gain, inflammation and ultimately, poor health.

You're much better off sticking to the good stuff. Natural sources of fat such as coconuts, olive oil, avocados, oily fish, nuts and seeds, egg yolks and grass-fed meat are all brilliant and I use them a lot throughout this book. They're high in vitamins A and D and keep you full for ages. However, you still need to be sensible about the amount of fat you consume – there needs to be a balance in the foods you eat.

## SO WHAT SHOULD I EAT?

I know it sounds as if there isn't anything left to eat once you've taken away the highly processed stuff but there are so many delicious things you can create with natural, wholesome foods. I never thought I'd be enjoying chocolate & hazelnut truffles (see page 195), seriously delicious fajitas (see page 127) and a tall, fluffy

## THE DANGERS OF SUGAR

Over the past few years, the dangers of consuming refined and processed sugars have become more and more obvious. The average British teenager consumes more than 500g (that's half a bag!) of added, refined sugar a week, and, while that may seem like a lot, it's often hidden by food manufacturers in everything from sliced bread to ketchup and so-called 'healthy' cereal bars. Watch out for sneakily concealed sugar in shop-bought savoury foods like soups, and avoid low-fat and 'diet' foods, which are pumped with refined sugar to replace the fat. It might not even be labelled as sugar: sweeteners, concentrated fruit juice, dextrose, maltose, aspartame, high-fructose corn syrup and evaporated cane juice are all best avoided. Check page 19 for better alternatives, but remember that even 'natural' sugars should be enjoyed in moderation; after all, sugar is sugar!

stack of delicious pancakes (see page 70) while eating this way, but these dishes can all be part of a healthier lifestyle and help you feel fantastic. This chapter will give you an explanation of the staple foods that I like to incorporate and some guidance about how to enjoy them. I've also included some information about ingredients I can't eat but which are healthy.

### • VEGGIES

Vegetables certainly don't have to be bland or boring and they should make up a large part of your diet. Try to fit in at least a few servings spread throughout the day's meals in order to get a wide and varied range of nutrients and minerals. My favourite way to do this is to enjoy a huge salad for lunch (see the salad guide on page 92) and snack on crunchy veg like cucumber and radishes dipped in homemade pesto (see page 248) throughout the day.

Green, leafy vegetables like spinach, kale, rocket and watercress are fantastic in smoothies and salads, while starchier veg such as sweet potatoes can be roasted with a drizzle of healthy oil. You can easily make a big batch of pesto at the beginning of the week and slice up some vegetables such as carrots and celery to store in the fridge so that you have a fast and easy snack readily available. While it's true that veggies lose a little bit of their nutrient content when cut up in advance, storing them in an airtight container and eating them within 2 to 3 days will reduce this.

Avocados are one of my absolute favourite nutrient-dense snacks, and I often eat them simply mashed with fresh lemon juice and flaky salt, or in a salad. They're very high in healthy fats and vitamin E and are absolutely delicious. I also love all sorts of leafy greens, broccoli, cauliflower, mushrooms, courgettes, asparagus, sweet potatoes and carrots, but feel free to experiment with your own favourites. I find that steaming, sautéing and roasting are the best methods to ensure flavourful vegetables, and a sprinkling of fresh herbs and, if you need it, flaky salt on top really makes a difference.

I always have garlic, ginger, shallots and lemongrass on hand as well – they keep for ages and give loads of flavour to many recipes.

### • FRUIT

Seasonal fruit, (locally grown is always best), is not only absolutely delicious but is also full of vitamins making it a brilliant quick snack or dessert. That said, I always recommend eating

whole fruit, rather than fruit juice, because the fibre and water you ingest when you eat the whole fruit slow down the digestion process. Imagine your digestive tract as a pipe – if you pour fruit juice down it, all the sugar goes straight through and hits your digestive system in one go. It's easy to drink the fructose (fruit sugar) equivalent of five or six oranges in one tall glass of orange juice! But if you stuff a whole orange through a pipe, it'll take some time to go down so the fruit sugar hits the liver slowly and doesn't spike your blood sugar too much. Although fruit contains many vitamins and beneficial nutrients, its high sugar content means that one or two pieces of whole fruit a day are plenty. When sugar hits the liver extremely quickly and in huge amounts, it's directly converted to fat and over time could possibly lead to liver damage. It makes sense, really – you wouldn't eat six oranges in one go, so why would you drink the equivalent?

Enjoying your fruit with a serving of healthy fat such as nut butter, nut milk or coconut cream is a good idea. I absolutely love the combo of an apple slathered with almond butter as a fast, filling snack!

### NUTS AND SEEDS

Nuts and seeds make a fantastic snack and are great for adding texture to salads and desserts. I find that nuts taste much, much better when roasted; almonds, cashews and pumpkin seeds are my favourites, and I simply toss them with some spices and salt, spread them out on a baking tray, and bake them in a 180°C/350°F/gas 4 oven for 10 to 12 minutes. I love using pecans, hazelnuts and walnuts in desserts, while Brazil nuts should be eaten raw and are a brilliant source of selenium.

Be mindful of the amount of nuts you consume, though, as they're high in omega-6 fatty acids, so eating too many could contribute to inflammation in the body. It's best to stick to a small handful at a time.

### DAIRY, GRAINS AND LEGUMES

Although I don't eat them myself and they're not a big part of my recipes (more about this on page 6), dairy, grains and legumes are considered to be part of a balanced diet, so feel free to include these in your meals. My way of eating might be slightly different to what works for you, but I think we can all agree that the most important thing is to eat a more unprocessed, colourful and healthy diet.

### HEALTHY FATS AND OILS

Vegetable and seed oils like sunflower oil, soybean oil, peanut oil and corn oil that you can buy at the supermarket go through an extraction process involving bleaching, deodorizing and hydrogenation, using harsh and toxic chemicals. I'm sure you'll agree that doesn't sound too great! They are also very high in inflammatory omega-6 fatty acids and go yucky quickly at room temperature, so they are prone to damage. For this reason, it's best to stick to unrefined, cold-pressed organic olive oil, rapeseed oil and nut oils as well as my personal favourite, coconut oil.

Coconut oil is a healthy saturated fat with plenty of medium-chain fatty acids which stays stable at high heats, making it perfect and very versatile as a cooking fat.

### SUSTAINABLE, HIGH-WELFARE MEAT AND FISH

Sustainable, ethically raised meat and poultry contain high amounts of vitamin B12, vitamin D3, iron and zinc, while oily fish is high in healthy omega-3 fatty acids, which are necessary for brain health and disease prevention. It's incredibly important to source the best meat you can; along with purchasing locally raised meat and poultry if possible, try to ensure that you know the animal has been humanely raised, well fed, and has lived a happy life. If you're able to, support local farmers and butchers. Not only is the quality of their meat and poultry a whole lot better than that of the average supermarket, but it's a really great way to support your local community.

Although high-welfare meats, poultry and fish are more expensive than their conventional counterparts, the knowledge that the meat you eat has been raised humanely and ethically means that it is very much worth it. I think that eating a smaller serving of sustainable meat or fish less often is far better than eating enormous portions of mass produced meat multiple times a day, and I encourage you to look at it in the same way. By buying cheaper cuts of meat and utilizing bones to make stock, you're not only saving money and preventing waste but honouring the animal by making use of every bit of it.

## WHAT DO LABELS MEAN?

I know it can be very confusing trying to find out exactly what you're buying, especially when it comes to meat, poultry and seafood. You might be surprised to learn that some of these terms are a bit misleading, so have a read through so that you're more informed about the best choice the next time you go shopping.

### GRASS-FED OR PASTURED

These terms mean that the animals have had plenty of space to roam and graze on a natural diet as they were biologically meant to. For beef and lamb, look for grass-fed meat – it's not only a much more natural and ethical way to raise the animals, but the meat contains many more nutrients, especially omega-3s, so it's a healthier choice for you as well. When it comes to poultry, pork and eggs, look for pastured, outdoor-reared meats and eggs, which means that the animals have foraged naturally for insects and plants and have been raised on the pastures outside. You might not spot these labels at your average supermarket, though – the best source for this kind of meat and eggs is a local farmer or butcher.

### ORGANIC

This means that the animals have been raised in a certified organic environment and fed certified organic feed for their entire life. The animals can't be fed antibiotics, artificial hormones or any genetically modified products, but they are often fed corn, soy or grain-based feed, which is not always their natural diet. The organic label also doesn't guarantee that the animals have been treated humanely (they might still be fed an excessive amount of food to 'bulk' them up before slaughter, for example), but it's a good option.

### FREE-RANGE

Unfortunately, this is a bit of a misleading one! According to the law, free-range means that the chickens and birds must have access to open-air runs in the daytime, for at least half of their lives. There aren't any strict regulations about the quality or size of the outside areas or the quality of their feed, but it's still a better choice than battery-farmed poultry.

### FISH

The oily varieties of fish such as salmon, trout, mackerel and sardines, are essential to a healthy diet because of their omega-3 fatty acid profile. I try to buy sustainable, wild-caught seafood and fish certified by the Marine Stewardship Council (MSC). Farmed fish, especially salmon, has been found to be contaminated with toxic pollutants, so it's best to go for wild-caught if you can.

## A BIT ABOUT OMEGAS

I've mentioned them a few times so far, and you might be wondering exactly what they are! Omega-3 and omega-6 fats are polyunsaturated fats that our bodies can't naturally produce, so it's important to include them in your diet. Things rich in omega-3s include oily fish, walnuts and flaxseed, while things rich in omega-6s include meat, poultry and eggs. Both are important to eat, but it's also important to keep a balance between the two. The best way to do this is to limit processed foods and make sure you eat oily fish at least twice a week.

## NATURAL SWEETENERS

When you reduce your consumption of processed and packaged foods, it can be tempting to replace the enormous amount of sugar they contain with 'healthier' desserts containing a truckload of 'natural' sugars, but the truth is that sugar is sugar, no matter what form it takes; I don't feel that simply replacing white, refined sugar with enormous amounts of natural sweeteners is the answer.

Instead, use them in moderation and try to stick to a maximum of two or three teaspoons of natural sweeteners a few times a week – these include pure maple syrup, coconut sugar, local honey and dates. Over time, you'll find that your cravings for sugar will decrease as your body adjusts. I do use natural sweeteners throughout this book in order to give sweetness to the dessert and treat recipes, but I've tried to keep the sugars to a minimum; remember, too, that the treat recipes should be occasional indulgences rather than everyday fare.

## HERBS AND SPICES

Fresh herbs and spices can truly transform a dish. They provide amazing flavours and are one of the easiest ways to switch up your favourite staples when you're getting a little tired of them! My favourite fresh herbs are parsley, coriander, dill, mint, thyme, chives, sage and basil, and the great thing about herbs is that they're not only readily available at supermarkets and farmers' markets, but they're also very easy to grow yourself, even if you have black thumbs like me!

When it comes to spices, my must-haves include black pepper, unrefined sea salt or Himalayan pink salt, dried oregano, dried thyme, garlic powder, roasted curry powder, chilli powder, ground cumin, ground cinnamon, nutmeg and ground cloves. I also love spice blends (make sure they don't contain any other odd ingredients, though), or you can make your own rubs and blends using the recipes on page 39. You'll also want to make sure that your dried herbs and spices are still fresh, as they start to lose their flavour after about two years.

## DRINKS

It goes without saying that you should try to avoid fizzy, artificially flavoured and coloured soft drinks, due to their high amounts of sugar and artificial sweeteners. Stick to water (still or sparkling) and herbal teas instead – you can always liven a glass of water up with fresh herbs and fresh fruit!

*tip*

When your cupboards fill up with lots of bags of various sizes and colours with all sorts of healthful ingredients, things can get a little disorganized! I keep my ingredients in glass jars labelled with reusable chalkboard stickers – they not only look nice, but also keep everything tidy and help me see what I've got.

# HOW TO SHOP LOCALLY AND SEASONALLY

Eating in season and shopping locally sounds like it'll be very expensive and difficult to do, but it's actually very easy and will help you minimize waste. It'll also ensure that the food you eat is at its peak and tastes incredible!

Fresh produce is best sourced from a local farmers' market or through a local box scheme – this way, you'll be receiving the freshest produce just days or even hours after it has been picked, and you'll also be receiving only the ripest produce at that time of year. It often works out a lot cheaper than buying fruit and veg from the supermarket, as there's much less packaging and hardly any travel costs; a lot of supermarket produce is picked long before it's ripe and travels thousands of miles before it reaches the shop. Buying British produce not only supports your local economy and farmers but may also mean you're contributing to a more sustainable farming future, so it's the best choice for everyone. If you're having a hard time finding a local farm that has fresh produce boxes, you can use the search tool on the Soil Association website to help you – www.soilassociation.org/boxschemes. There are some online providers of them as well, although these can be slightly more expensive and often contain produce imported from other countries. If supermarkets are your only available option, try to stick to British produce and avoid foods that have travelled thousands of miles to get to your plate (you can find out where fruit and vegetables have been imported from on the label). Fresh produce will naturally be cheaper when it's in season, as well, so use the chart below to help you eat frugally and seasonally.

| winter | spring | summer | autumn |
|---|---|---|---|
| SQUASH | ASPARAGUS | LEAFY GREENS | PUMPKINS |
| CAULIFLOWER | BROCCOLI | BEETS | CRANBERRIES |
| KALE | CAULIFLOWER | BROCCOLI | POMEGRANATES |
| SWEET | GREEN BEANS | LETTUCE | APPLES |
| POTATOES | PEAS | CUCUMBERS | ARTICHOKES |
| BRUSSELS | SPINACH | TOMATOES | LEAFY GREENS |
| SPROUTS | ROCKET | AUBERGINES | BRUSSELS |
| BOK CHOY | WATERCRESS | COURGETTES | SPROUTS |
| WATERCRESS | LEAFY GREENS | RADISHES | KALE |
| ROCKET | AVOCADOS | PEAS | PARSNIPS |
| SPINACH | CHERRIES | PEPPERS | CARROTS |
| PARSNIPS | RHUBARB | AVOCADOS | PEPPERS |
| CARROTS | FIGS | BERRIES | WINTER SQUASH |
| CABBAGE | PLUMS | FIGS | SWEET |
| APPLES | | GRAPES | POTATOES |
| PEARS | | MELONS | |
| POMEGRANATES | | STONE FRUIT | |
| PINEAPPLES | | | |

When it comes to meat, poultry and eggs, purchasing them directly from a local farmer or farm shop/health food shop is the best option, but if you're not able to do this, a high-quality butcher or sourcing online are great alternatives. Sustainable and seasonal seafood is something that your local fishmonger should be able to help you with, and good fishmongers as well as supermarket fish counters should have the freshest locally caught fish. Try to stick to wild-caught or line-caught varieties rather than farmed ones, and try to ensure that the fish you buy has been certified by the Marine Stewardship Council (MSC).

## • FISH SEASONS

### WHITE FISH
Cod, haddock, sole, plaice, halibut and hake, crab, mussels, clams, prawns and other shellfish are in season throughout the summer, autumn and winter months, but not in the spring.

### OILY FISH
Wild salmon, mackerel, sardines and sea trout are generally in season throughout the summer and autumn months. Use tinned or frozen versions instead in the winter and spring.

# STOCKING UP AND SIMPLE TIPS

There might be some ingredients used in the book that you're not familiar with and are not sure where to get, so I've described the ingredients I use often below, along with some tips on where to find them.

You'll notice that I tend to use the same staple ingredients quite a bit throughout the book – this is because I want to keep things simple and accessible for everyone. By keeping the number of 'unusual' ingredients limited, I want to make sure that you won't have to pay extortionate prices for a tiny jar of something that you'll end up never using again! Everything other than the ingredients below (and including some of them!) should be readily available at your local supermarket.

## • COCONUT OIL

For use in baking and cooking, I like to use odourless coconut oil, which has been lightly steamed to remove the coconut smell and taste – this lets other flavours shine through. I tend to use a 'cuisine' coconut oil from Biona Organics.

Odourless oils are perfect for cooking and baking, as there's no coconutty aftertaste. Buying coconut oil in small jars at supermarkets or health food shops is often ridiculously expensive, so I recommend having a look online to see if you can purchase a bigger quantity for a much better price!

## • COCONUT MILK AND CREAM

These two are dairy-free lifesavers. Full-fat coconut milk is used throughout the book – it can be used as the base for delicious ice cream (see page 216), is brilliant for adding a creamy, oriental touch to sauces (see pages 116, 147), and is amazing when added to a smoothie. I always use the full-fat tinned version. Make sure

the brand you buy is organic, preferably, and contains only water and coconut; any other ingredients are unnecessary and could lead to my recipes not working properly.

Coconut cream is the thick, white layer of cream that forms at the top of a tin of coconut milk when placed in the fridge. To separate the coconut cream from the layer of coconut water, simply pop a can of coconut milk into the fridge overnight, or for at least 8 hours, then open the can, scoop out the thick white part and place it in a bowl – that's it! Use the leftover water in smoothies. To make coconut whipped cream for use in desserts or just to serve with fresh berries, follow the directions on page 256.

## • RAW NUTS

Although you can buy them at almost any supermarket in the 'baking' aisle, it can be a lot cheaper and easier to purchase these in bigger bags online or at a health food shop. I buy 500g or 1kg bags of organic raw nuts online and use them in recipes, roast them for snacks, and turn them into nut milk or nut butter.

## • GROUND ALMONDS

I use these in most of my baking. Ground almonds, sometimes known as almond flour, contain calcium and have a nutty flavour. It's made by grinding blanched raw almonds (almonds which have had their skins removed) into a fine powder, and it's very versatile, which means you can use it in anything from baking to making a crunchy topping for fish. Try to get a very finely ground version for the best results. Ground almonds are very high in omega-6 fatty acids, though, so should not be consumed in large quantities on a daily basis.

If you or someone you know is intolerant of or allergic to almonds (or if you want a cheaper alternative!), you can easily replace the ground almonds in any of my recipes with an equal amount of homemade sunflower seed flour. To make this, place a large bag of hulled sunflower seeds in a food processor and grind until very fine for about 3 minutes. Sieve the flour twice, then store in an airtight container for up to 2 months. It doesn't have the same nutty flavour as ground almonds, but it's a great alternative, especially in my cracker recipe (see page 253). Do be wary of using it in a recipe that calls for bicarbonate of soda or baking powder, though – the chemical reaction between the sunflower seeds and the raising agent turns your product green, and, although it's perfectly safe to eat, might look a little unappealing!

### • ARROWROOT

This is made from the root of the arrowroot plant and is easily digestible. It adds a soft, light texture to baked goods, so I use it quite a bit in cakes, cookies and breads. Ensure you buy a version with no sulphites; I recommend having a look online for the best deals.

If you can't find arrowroot, you can use tapioca starch or potato starch instead. Tapioca is extracted from the root of the cassava plant, and potato starch is simply the starch from a potato! As these are all root starches, they tend to be interchangeable, so use whatever is most easily available to you. You will probably be able to purchase both tapioca and potato starch at a local health food shop.

### • COCONUT FLOUR

Coconut flour is made from dried ground coconut meat, and it's very high in fibre and protein. It is extremely absorbent and can be difficult to work with, so I would not advise replacing it in any recipes! Since I only use a small amount in my baked goods to provide texture, a bag will last you quite a while. You can buy it in most health food shops or order it online.

### • COCONUT SUGAR

Coconut sugar is a granulated sugar made from the sap of the blossoms of the coconut palm. It's dark brown in colour and unrefined, and has a lovely caramel taste. It provides very small quantities of iron, magnesium, zinc, potassium and amino acids, and as it has a lower glycaemic index than white table sugar, it causes a less dramatic spike in blood sugar. However, it's still a sugar and should be used sparingly. I purchase mine online, as it's often extortionately priced in shops! If you can't find it or it's not within your means, raw cane sugar can be bought at most supermarkets and will work in all my recipes.

### • COCONUT AMINOS

This is a salty, soy-free seasoning sauce made from coconut palm sap. It tastes great and I use it in dressings and meals as a soy sauce substitute. You can purchase it online, or you can use gluten-free tamari instead.

### • HONEY

Raw, local and unfiltered honey contains live enzymes and is antibacterial. It's brilliant for coughs and colds. The darker the colour, the stronger the flavour, so if you're not a huge fan of the flavour of raw honey, try to source a lighter-coloured one (but make sure it hasn't been pasteurized, clarified or filtered, as these remove its benefits – baking with honey will also do this due to the high heat. I use it to add a little sweetness to herbal tea or to drizzle over chia seed puddings. Try to source from a local farmers' market, or buy raw honey from the supermarket.

### • MAPLE SYRUP

I adore maple syrup – it's full of minerals such as manganese, zinc and potassium. It also raises blood sugar more slowly than refined sugar, but keep in mind that it should be enjoyed in moderation, as it is still a form of sugar. Make sure that you're buying pure maple syrup rather than maple-flavoured syrup, which is often full of refined sugar syrups and artificial maple flavouring!

## • DATES

Dates are grown on date palms and are soft, sticky and absolutely delicious. I use them as a binder in some of my treat recipes, but I also love them as a snack, stuffed with almond butter (see page 207). There are generally two types of dates – hard, dried dates and softer dates, and both are readily available in supermarkets. I use the soft, squishy Medjool dates in my recipes, but if you only have dried dates to hand, simply soak them in some boiling water for a few minutes until they soften and proceed with the recipe.

## • CACAO

The difference between 'cacao' and 'cocoa' is very confusing, but cacao generally means that unroasted cocoa beans have been ground up to produce it, while cocoa powder is the roasted version of cacao. Still with me? Essentially, they're the same product, but cocoa has been roasted, while cacao is the raw, unroasted version. Both contain plenty of monounsaturated fats, antioxidants and magnesium, and they can be used interchangeably. Although the raw cacao is slightly higher in antioxidants, roasted cocoa powder is still a very nutritious and beneficial food, and many people (including me) prefer the flavour of the roasted version, so use whatever you prefer or can easily source. Another thing to consider is that raw cacao is a lot more expensive than cocoa powder. Whatever you choose, make sure you're buying a Fairtrade powder and not a mix that contains refined sugar and icky milk powders – a quick look on the ingredients list will tell you this (it should only contain cacao).

I've also used cacao butter in my homemade chocolate recipe (see page 40). Cacao butter is the healthy fat from the cacao bean and has a rich, buttery, chocolatey flavour. It smells incredible as well! Buy it online rather than in shops, as it's so much cheaper, and try to purchase a Fairtrade version to help support small family cacao farms.

## • DARK CHOCOLATE

Although I do give a recipe for homemade dark chocolate (see page 41), any high-quality dark chocolate will work in my recipes. I try to stick to bars made without refined sugars, but anything with a 70% cacao percentage or higher is fine. For baking, I absolutely love the dark chocolate chips and drops from Real Food Source, which contain only organic cacao and organic coconut sugar. They're very reasonably priced, taste incredible and are made from great ingredients.

## • VANILLA

I think vanilla is such an underrated ingredient! I use it in almost every treat recipe in the form of either homemade vanilla extract (see page 261) or vanilla bean powder. Vanilla bean powder, which I like to use in raw desserts and smoothies, can be purchased online, and although it might seem quite expensive, a little really does go a long way; a small packet will last you months of daily use.

## NECESSARY KITCHEN EQUIPMENT

The vast majority of the things in this book can be made with just a few simple pieces of equipment. Your kitchen really doesn't need to be crammed with expensive gadgets in order to produce delicious food, but having a few basic kitchen tools will help make cooking easier, faster and much more efficient. You can purchase these at most large supermarkets or at specialist cooking shops like Lakeland.

1. A FEW GOOD, SHARP KNIVES – You'll use these for almost anything you do in the kitchen, and investing in a set of good, sharp knives will save you hours of frustration. A large chef's knife is best for chopping most vegetables and meat, and a small paring knife is very useful for finely chopping garlic and fresh herbs. You'll also want to buy a vegetable peeler if you don't have one already – it's simple but invaluable!

2. STAINLESS STEEL POTS AND PANS – I recommend having a frying pan, a medium saucepan and a large pot – these basics will cover everything from a fried egg to a pot of soup. Make sure you have a large wooden spoon, stainless steel tongs and a spatula to use with them as well as an oven mitt. A ceramic non-stick frying pan is also handy and involves less washing up – always a good thing!

3. MEASURING TOOLS –You might have noticed that I use volume measurements throughout the book as well as the usual weights. This is because I want everyone to be able to make these recipes, even if you don't have weighing scales or are completely new to cooking. Of course, all values are given in gramme weights too, so you can use those if you

prefer. I recommend buying a set of measuring cups as well as a set of measuring spoons – measuring cups are very helpful for cooking and baking, while the spoons are essential for measuring spices and small amounts. I prefer the metal versions to the silicone ones because of their durability, and make sure that they're clearly marked so that you don't confuse your teaspoons with your tablespoons!

### 4. BOWLS AND CHOPPING BOARDS –
A few glass and stainless steel bowls of different sizes will be incredibly useful for mixing doughs, tossing salads and storing leftovers. Wooden chopping boards are best, as they last longer than plastic ones. Make sure you use a separate board for preparing raw meat and fish.

### 5. A BAKING SHEET AND MUFFIN TRAY – A 27 x 35cm metal baking sheet can
be used for absolutely everything. You might also want to purchase a smaller square baking tin, a round cake tin and a loaf tin. A muffin tray can be used for everything from breakfasts to desserts, and if you're short on space, you can turn any of my cake recipes into cupcakes or muffins as well, to save you having to buy any more baking tins. Make sure you have plenty of parchment paper and paper muffin cups as well, to save on washing up – I love the *If You Care* brand, as it's unbleached and made from recycled paper.

### 6. BLENDER OR HAND-HELD BLENDER
– Blenders and hand-held stick blenders are so versatile and useful. I use mine primarily to make smoothies, soups and sauces. Although countertop blenders are often very powerful and will whizz things into a smooth mixture in seconds, they can take up a lot of space and are often very expensive. I'd advise getting a good hand-held blender, as they're much more convenient and easy to store, and between that and a food processor, there's very little you can't do!

### 7. FOOD PROCESSOR – My food processor
is definitely the most utilized gadget in my kitchen! From making nut butters or whizzing up a batch of homemade pesto to chopping vegetables, I use it for absolutely everything. I love and highly recommend Magimix ones, as they last for decades and are very easy to clean, but if they're not in your price range, there are many other brands to choose from. Make sure you pick one that has a small bowl as well as a large one in addition to various sizes of grating/ slicing blades; you can even purchase food processors that double as blenders and hand-held blenders to save more space.

## • KNIFE SKILLS

If you're new to cooking, one of the most important things to learn is how to use a knife properly.

1. Hold the knife by pinching the blade between your thumb and first finger, then wrapping the rest of your fingers around the handle of the knife. This will give you the most control.

2. With your other hand, curl your fingers and your thumb into a 'claw' over the ingredients, so that if the knife slips, it will hit your knuckles rather than your fingertips.

3. Always cut a flat surface on the object you're chopping so that it rests flatly on the chopping board and can't slip. For example, when you're cutting an apple, slice horizontally across the bottom in order to make a flat surface so that when you slice it, the apple doesn't roll around or slip.

There are a few different types of cuts and ways to chop – I've described a few of the ones frequently used below.

SLICE – First cut a flat surface on one side as described to the left, then cut the vegetable into thin slices with vertical cuts.

DICE – This means to cut into cubes. Slice the vegetable, then cut the slices into thick sticks using vertical cuts. Slice these thick sticks into cubes by cutting horizontally across. For a fine dice, simply cut into thinner sticks and smaller cubes.

JULIENNE – This means to cut into thin sticks. First slice the food, usually a vegetable, into thin pieces, then cut each thin piece into small sticks using vertical cuts.

CHIFFONADE – A fancy name for rolling and slicing leafy greens or herbs into thin, pretty ribbons for garnish. Simply stack up the leaves, roll them up tightly into a cigar shape, and slice crosswise, starting at one end of the roll of leaves and working towards the other end, to create thin ribbons.

FINELY CHOP – Roughly chop first, and repeat until you have very, very fine pieces.

## FOOD ON THE GO

Packing meals and snacks for school, work, travel, days out and holidays doesn't have to be difficult. With some preparation, you can enjoy a healthy diet wherever you are.

For a day away, I try to pack a meal, two snacks and a drink, preferably in glass or BPA-free plastic containers (don't forget the cutlery!). When you're travelling or taking things with you, avoid foods that need refrigeration and juicy foods, as they might go soggy. Pack salad dressings, sauces and dips in jars with the lids tightly screwed on so they don't leak, and pop them into a resealable bag just in case they do. Always throw in a lemon wedge to squeeze over vegetables and salads to brighten them up.

I tend to take meals that don't have too many components, so they're easy to eat — usually, it'll be a salad and all I have to do is drizzle over the dressing, or I'll bring along leftovers of sweet potato pad Thai (see page 122), beef curry (see page 148) or salmon patties with spiced cauliflower rice (see page 124).

For snacks, I usually take roasted nuts or seeds, a home-made muffin, an energy bar or sliced vegetables with a dip, depending on what I have prepared. Having a well-stocked cupboard and freezer makes this very easy — I simply grab a handful of spicy seeds (see page 15) from the jar on the counter, and a carrot, coconut and pineapple walnut streusel muffin (see page 57) from the freezer and I'm done!

When it comes to drinks, I've always got a water bottle with me and will often throw in a sprig of mint and some frozen berries in the morning that will infuse the water throughout the day. You can also bring your morning smoothies with you in a travel mug — if you have the chance, a squeeze of lemon from the wedge in your lunchbox will freshen the smoothie up. If I'm travelling or facing a particularly busy day, I also make sure to eat a very big breakfast, and pack my smoothies with extra fats like almond butter and coconut milk.

## HOW TO PREPARE AND PLAN MEALS

Planning and preparing your meals and snacks in advance is absolutely the best way to help you eat well. If you've got a container of cut-up veggies along with a jar of pesto in the fridge, a stash of muffins or hazelnut butter fudge at the back of the freezer and some spicy roasted nuts in the cupboard, you're a lot less likely to grab a chocolate bar or biscuits when you're in need of a snack! When you first start preparing everything from scratch, it might seem like there's a lot to do and you might be worried about having to spend hours in the kitchen every day, but it definitely doesn't have to be that way if you take a spare hour or two on the weekend, blast some music, and plan and prep for the week ahead using these simple steps. Over time, you'll find your own way of setting yourself up for eating healthfully, so feel free to adapt this plan to what suits you best. You might have some extras by the end of the week – if you freeze these in portions, you'll prevent wastage and you'll soon build up a varied collection of things in your freezer to choose from when you want a very speedy dinner!

1 I always like to plan out the week's meals before going shopping to save on food waste — it's really easy and will prevent any 'what can we have for dinner tonight' emergencies. Pick and choose from the meals in this book, have a look online for inspiration, or keep it simple and choose a protein (along with a spice blend or rub to liven things up — see page 39) and add a variety of veg. Once I've worked out what we'll need for the week's dinners, I'll decide what snacks or breakfasts I'm making and check on my supplies to make sure I'm not running low on anything before heading off to the market and shops with a list in hand.

2 Once you get home, whack the oven on and roast a batch or two of spiced nuts or seeds, following the instructions on page 15. You can also pop some raw almonds into a bowl and cover them with boiling water to soak while you do everything else, if you'd like to make a batch of almond milk (see page 40). Set the roasted nuts aside to make nut butter once they're cool, or pop them into a glass jar for snacking throughout the week.

3 While the oven is hot, mix up the batter for some cookies, muffins or a hearty loaf (I love my crunchy nut banana loaf, page 189) and bake, or make a batch of crackers (see page 253). You can also throw in a frittata (see page 60) if you'd like to sort out your breakfasts for a day or two, or add a tray of meatballs (see page 136) or chicken thighs with a spice blend (see page 39) to easily add protein to salads and meals. While all that is in the oven, whizz up a few butters or sauces to add flavour and variety to meals; I tend to make a nut butter, a pesto, and two types of dressings and store them in glass jars in the fridge to use throughout the week. You might also want to stir up a batch of freezer fudge (see page 192) or nut & date bites (see page 198) while the food processor is in use!

4 Chop and prepare your veg — I find that if I make plenty of veggie sticks to snack on, wash produce for salads and meals, and cut up an array of fruit and veg to grab for smoothies in the mornings, it makes it much easier to fit in loads of vitamin- and mineral-rich produce on busy weekdays. If you're the type of person who loves ice-cold smoothies, you can throw some of the fruit and veg into glass containers in the freezer as well and use it throughout the week.

5 As you're chopping away anyway, I recommend cutting up some more veg to make a quick big pot of soup for dinner — easy clean-up, and any extras make a delicious lunch with a bit of pesto stirred in! While you simmer the soup, hard-boil a handful of eggs (pop them into a pan of boiling water for 10 minutes, then plunge into cold water) and keep them in a container in the fridge for up to 2 days as an easy and very nutritious addition to breakfasts and salads.

6 And lastly … blend the almond milk if making (recipe on page 40), slice up any loaves, frittatas or treats into pieces to freeze, and make sure everything is in a labelled container — this'll help you tell what's what!

# A FEW QUICK TIPS BEFORE YOU GET STARTED

These little things will save you a lot of time and frustration as you cook through the book!

- When halving a recipe, always rewrite the recipe with halved quantities before you begin. I can't tell you how many times I've ruined dishes because I added full amounts of some ingredients and halved amounts of others – it's easy to get distracted and mix things up. Besides, nobody wants to be dealing with fractions in the middle of cooking!

- When you're freezing fresh fruit or veg, wash them, lay them out in a single layer on a baking tray and pop into the freezer for an hour or two, until the outside is just frozen. Then transfer to an airtight container or a resealable bag. This prevents you getting enormous lumps of frozen fruit and makes it much easier to defrost.

- Doubling or tripling a recipe, especially when it comes to healthy baking, doesn't always work out – you'll have to experiment with the quantities and baking time if you choose to do this. I recommend sticking with the original quantities I've used and making the recipe twice, separately, if you need double the amount.

# THE BASICS

## • COOKING METHODS

Learning how to use a few of these basic cooking techniques will give you the skills you need to rustle up a quick meal easily, with or without a recipe – as long as you've got a few ingredients on hand and some herbs or spices, you can make a beautiful dinner in minutes by combining a few different techniques and flavour combinations.

There are certain cooking methods that pair up with certain foods. You wouldn't sauté cookies or steam a steak, and there are good reasons for that! All these methods have individual characteristics, and knowing how and when to use each one is the first step towards making a really great plate of food.

**SAUTÉING** – This means to fry something in a little bit of oil in a very hot pan. It's important to heat up the pan for a minute, then add your oil or fat of choice before heating that up for a minute as well, so that the food sizzles when it hits the pan. When you sauté, keep tossing or moving the food with your spatula so that it cooks evenly. Sautéing is perfect for leafy greens, quick-cooking pieces of meat and fish, and for building up lots of flavour in vegetables before you make a soup or stew.

**STEAMING** – I tend not to steam vegetables very often, as they can taste a little bland and can become overcooked and mushy if cooked for just a few minutes too long. However, steaming can be useful to cook vegetables quickly and easily if you're in a pinch and especially useful for roots. Steaming conserves nutrients such as vitamins B and C as the ingredients are cooked quickly and there's no leakage into the water.

**BRAISING** – This means to first sauté meat or vegetables over a gentle heat before adding a liquid such as water or stock and covering the pot. This way, you get flavour from initially sautéing, yet the vegetables or meat cook until completely tender thanks to the added liquid, so braising is perfect for tougher, thicker cuts of meat and slightly sturdier vegetables. Use a saucepan or casserole pan and heat it up, then add your oil or fat and heat just as if you were sautéing. Add your meat or vegetables and cook until lightly browned on all sides, then add just a little bit of liquid – you don't want to immerse what you're cooking, so I suggest adding enough liquid to cover it about a quarter of the way up. Reduce the heat to low, cover the pan with a lid and cook until tender.

**ROASTING** – Roasting meat and vegetables at a high heat results in crisp outsides and tender insides, and it's this contrast in texture along with the caramelization which takes place that makes roasting one of my absolute favourite cooking methods. Just whack up the oven to about 200°C/400°F/gas 6, toss your vegetables or rub your meat with oil, salt and any spices you'd like to add, then roast until golden on the outside and cooked on the inside.

**SIMMERING AND BOILING** – There's a big difference between boiling and simmering. Boiling refers to the stage at which bubbles rapidly and violently break the surface of the liquid, while simmering describes just a few small bubbles gently popping up. Simmering cooks food gently and delicately, so it's perfect for soups and stews. Boiling is great for eggs and root vegetables.

## • COOKING VEGETABLES

Different types of vegetables are best cooked in different ways to maximize nutrients as well as flavour. Leafy greens are best when served raw in a salad or sautéd with some chopped garlic or lemon juice. Root vegetables like carrots, beets, potatoes, sweet potatoes and parsnips can be steamed or roasted, while less starchy veg like broccoli, cauliflower, peppers, peas, aubergines, bok choy and green beans are best steamed or sliced quite thinly and sautéd in a little oil.

Soups are brilliant for using up all kinds of vegetables – however, remember that the finished dish depends on the quality of the ingredients: in other words, you get what you put in, so limp celery and soft, bendy carrots won't do it. It's incredibly simple – sauté leeks, carrots, a chopped clove of garlic and a diced onion in oil for a few minutes. Add a splash of water and cover the pot for 5 to 10 minutes in order to draw out all their flavour, then add a variety of vegetables, making sure to add the sturdier ones like carrots and sweet potatoes at the beginning and any leafy greens at the last minute so that they don't lose their vibrancy. If you'd like a thick soup, add a medium potato or sweet potato, or stick with greens, tomatoes and peppers for a lighter soup. Cover the vegetables with stock (or a mixture of hot water and a homemade stock cube, see pages 76–79) and simmer until all the vegetables are tender. You can also toss in a pinch of spice – cumin and smoked paprika are very warming and work well with flavours like tomato soup, while lemongrass and fresh ginger go well with lighter soups and stocks to give them an oriental flavour – add these at the sauté stage. Blend or keep the soup chunky – it's your choice!

## • COOKING MEAT, POULTRY AND FISH

There are so many different cuts that it can definitely feel a little overwhelming when you're trying to choose what would work best in a recipe or what would be the easiest to cook, but hopefully this page will give you a little guidance when it comes to all the different ways to cook meat, poultry and fish.

The fastest things to get on the table tend to be quick-cooking cuts like skinless, boneless chicken breasts or thighs, beef steaks or strips, minced meats or fillets of fish. These are best sautéd, whole or sliced into thin pieces, and either served with a sauce or tossed with sautéd vegetables. Very thin fillets of fish such as sole are best quickly pan-fried and served with lemon and sautéd vegetables, while thicker fillets such as wild salmon or hake are better baked or grilled.

Tougher and more inexpensive cuts such as beef flank, brisket, rump and shank, pork or lamb shoulder and chicken legs are definitely best braised for quite a while in a flavourful sauce or stock so that they become tender.

There are so many different ways to add flavour to whatever type of cut you choose to cook, from sauces to marinades to spice rubs – here are a few basic recipes to try out!

### LEMON–GARLIC CHICKEN MARINADE:

Combine 60ml (¼ cup) of olive oil, 4 chopped cloves of garlic, a teaspoon of dried oregano, a teaspoon of salt, ½ teaspoon of pepper, and the zest of 1 lemon in a resealable bag. Add 4 skinless, boneless chicken breasts or thighs, toss them around in the marinade, seal the bag and let the chicken marinate in the fridge for up to an hour before cooking.

### SPICY PAPRIKA & CAYENNE BEEF RUB:

Stir together 1 tablespoon of paprika, ½ teaspoon each of salt, pepper, coconut sugar, garlic powder, onion powder and cayenne powder, then rub over beef strips or flank, brisket, rump or shank roasts before grilling, sautéing or braising.

### THAI BEEF MARINADE:

In a resealable bag, combine the juice of ½ a lime, ½ tablespoon of coconut sugar, ½ tablespoon of fish sauce, a teaspoon of sesame oil, a teaspoon of freshly grated ginger, and a finely chopped clove of garlic with steaks or strips of beef. Seal the bag and marinate in the fridge for about 2 hours.

### TOMATO & GARLIC BRAISING SAUCE:

Sauté a large cut of beef such as brisket, rump, or shank in a large casserole pot until browned all over, then remove from the pan and set aside. Now sauté a carrot, ½ a chopped onion, a teaspoon of dried thyme and 6 peeled whole cloves of garlic, and add a 400ml tin of chopped tomatoes once everything has browned. Stir, then add the beef, turn the heat down to very low, cover the pot and cook for 2 to 3 hours, until the beef is very tender.

### CORIANDER & CUMIN PORK RUB:

Combine ½ teaspoon of salt, ½ teaspoon of pepper, 2 teaspoons of ground cumin, ½ teaspoon of ground coriander and ½ teaspoon of chilli powder, and rub it over pork loin steaks or pork chops before grilling, sautéing or braising.

### ALMOND BUTTER SATAY SAUCE:

In a small saucepan, mix together 125g (½ cup) of almond butter, 1 chopped garlic clove, 60ml (¼ cup) of almond milk, ½ teaspoon of lime juice and ½ teaspoon of fish sauce and whisk constantly until hot. Serve as a dipping sauce for sautéd chicken or beef strips.

### SPICY TACO GROUND BEEF SEASONING:

In a small bowl, combine a tablespoon of chilli powder, a teaspoon of arrowroot, 1½ teaspoons of ground cumin, a teaspoon each of salt and pepper, ½ teaspoon of paprika, and ¼ teaspoon each of garlic powder, onion powder, crushed red pepper flakes and dried oregano. Put 750g of minced meat into a hot frying pan with a little oil, sauté for 3 to 4 minutes, add the taco seasoning and cook for 5 to 8 minutes, stirring constantly, until everything is evenly coated. Serve with a green salad, guacamole (see page 250) and homemade tortilla wraps (see page 254)!

### MUSTARD & DILL SAUCE:

Mix together 2 tablespoons of olive oil, a tablespoon of Dijon mustard, 2 tablespoons of chopped dill, the zest of ½ a lemon, and ½ teaspoon each of salt and pepper. Divide over 4 wild salmon or trout fillets and grill or bake the salmon fillets for about 10 minutes at 200°C/400°F/gas 6.

# HOMEMADE NUT BUTTERS AND NUT MILKS

Homemade nut butters and milks are some of the easiest and most rewarding things to make yourself. You can experiment with different flavours or combinations to find your favourite, and it takes hardly any time at all to whip up a batch!

## HOMEMADE NUT BUTTERS

I much prefer roasted nut butters to raw nut butters; roasted nut butter means that the nuts have been roasted to draw out their flavour before being blended, while raw butters are just raw nuts blended until smooth. When you're making nut butters, you'll want to use a high-powered blender (but you'll have to scrape down the sides quite often) or a robust food processor (the best choice) so that you get a creamy result. I recommend trying your hand at hazelnut butter first – it's the quickest and easiest.

To roast your nuts, spread them on a baking sheet and pop them into the oven for 10 to 15 minutes at 180°C/350°F/gas 4, until fragrant and golden. Transfer to a food processor or blender and whizz for about 10 to 15 minutes, until the nuts have transformed into a smooth butter. In the first few minutes, it'll look like ground-up nut flour, then, when the nuts release their oils, the mixture will start to come together into a very, very thick paste, or 'dough'. You might have to stop to scrape the sides a few times here. Keep going, as the paste will thin out to become a smooth nut butter. You want to process the nut butter until it's thin enough to drizzle off a spoon. That's it!

At this point, you can add any spices or flavourings – I love a sprinkle of cinnamon with almond or pecan butter, or try adding a few spoonfuls of cacao powder and a pitted date to hazelnut butter. You could even experiment with different combinations of nuts.

## NUT MILKS

Use about 150g (1 cup) of raw nuts (almonds and pecans are my favourites) and soak them in a bowl of boiling water for half an hour to an hour. They'll plump up and become very soft, so that they're easy to blend. Now drain them, rinse them under cold water, and put them into a blender along with about 750ml (3 cups) of cold water. Blend for about 2 minutes, until smooth and milky in colour, then taste. At this point, you can add whatever flavourings you'd like – I tend to add some vanilla bean powder, 2 or 3 dates for sweetness, and a dash of cinnamon, but you can use whatever you fancy! If you're going to use the almond milk for baking and savoury recipes, though, you'll want to leave it plain, just almonds and water.

Once you've made any additions, blend again to disperse them, then strain the nut milk into a bowl through an old tea towel, a piece of muslin cloth or a nut milk bag (you can get these very cheaply online). Squeeze and wring the cloth to extract any last drops of milk, then discard the solid pulp inside the cloth.

Transfer the milk to an airtight container, clip-top bottle or sealed jar and keep in the fridge for up to 4 days. It'll separate over time, so give it a good stir or shake before using or serving.

## MAKING YOUR OWN DARK CHOCOLATE

All you need is cacao powder, cacao butter, a bit of vanilla bean powder and a splash of maple syrup to make your own dark chocolate, and it's incredibly easy to do as well! Place 200g of cacao butter in a heatproof bowl and place over a pan of hot (but not boiling) water. Make sure that the bottom of the bowl does not come in contact with the water. Set the pan over a very low heat and wait, stirring occasionally, until the cacao butter has melted completely.

Lift the bowl from the pan and set it on the countertop, then add 75g (¾ cup) of cacao powder, a teaspoon of vanilla bean powder and 60ml (¼ cup) of maple syrup. Whisk very well, until smooth and shiny, then let the chocolate mixture sit for about an hour or two, until completely cooled.

Now transfer the mixture to silicone moulds or simply divide it between two or three rectangular containers to make 'bars' of chocolate. Place in the fridge to set. Store the homemade chocolate in the fridge, as it will melt at room temperature.

# THINGS TO GET OUT OF BED FOR

We all love hitting the snooze button, but rushing through your morning without having the chance to eat a proper breakfast isn't the best way to start your day. These recipes range from my go-to green smoothie which doesn't taste like pond water and make-ahead asparagus & tomato frittata slice for a grab-and-go option, to hazelnut and cacao waffles perfect for lazy, indulgent Sundays to help you start your day in a healthy, energizing way!

# THE PERFECT SMOOTHIE GUIDE

Make up your own combination with the help of this guide – feel free to experiment with flavours to find your favourite combination!

## 1 choose a liquid (250ml or 1 cup)

I tend to use a mixture of these – my favourite is half almond milk and half coconut milk. It's very creamy from the coconut but not too thick thanks to the almond milk. If you're choosing to include dairy, full-fat milk and yoghurt are also great options.

- almond milk
- coconut water
- coconut milk

## 2 add your greens (a very large handful)

I suggest using baby spinach or cucumber at first while you get used to drinking your greens, as they have a much milder, more mellow flavour!

- baby spinach
- cucumber
- kale

## 3 throw in some fruit (100g or 1 cup)

I like to use a mixture of half frozen fruit and half fresh fruit, as I like my smoothies ice-cold. Feel free to use any fruit you like, but these are my favourites.

- bananas
- apple
- nectarines or peaches
- pineapple
- berries
- cherries
- mango

## 4 finish it off with some add-ins (a small handful)

Just a small handful or spoonful of these can add so much flavour and texture – they'll really brighten up your smoothies! I usually add one or two of them, and I'm always experimenting with different combinations.

- fresh mint or parsley
- nut butters
- vanilla bean powder
- raw honey
- bee pollen
- chia seeds
- lemon juice

# 'DOESN'T TASTE LIKE POND WATER' GREEN SMOOTHIE

I know they're good for you, but a lot of shop-bought green smoothies don't taste very appealing – frankly, I find they taste a bit like pond water, which is where the name for this recipe comes from! They're often loaded with fruit sugars as well, so while this version may be a little less sweet, it's a lot better for you due to the lack of excessive fructose. I've used plenty of fresh mint and lemon juice to add lots of flavour as well.

*serves 1*

**10 MINUTES PREPARATION TIME**

250ml (1 cup) almond or full-fat milk
a large handful of baby spinach
1 frozen banana or 50g
   (½ cup) frozen pineapple
¼ of a cucumber
a very large handful of fresh
   mint leaves
1 tablespoon chia seeds
the juice of ½ a lemon

**OPTIONAL:**
50g (½ cup) frozen blueberries
   (these will turn your smoothie
   a gorgeous purple hue!)

1. Pour the almond milk into a powerful blender, then add all of the other ingredients.

2. Blend for a minute or two until completely smooth, with no chunks remaining. Enjoy!

# DECADENT COCONUT HOT CHOCOLATE

I've used both cacao powder and dark chocolate here for the ultimate chocolate hit – this hot chocolate is seriously rich! Thick and creamy, the coconut milk gives it a hint of lovely coconut flavour. Feel free to use another homemade nut milk instead of the almond milk if you like. This is a perfect weekend breakfast treat.

*serves 4*

10 MINUTES PREPARATION TIME

200ml (¾ cup) full-fat tinned
   coconut milk
125ml (½ cup) almond milk
1 heaped teaspoon cacao powder
1 heaped teaspoon coconut
   sugar or unrefined brown sugar
50g high-quality dark chocolate
   or dark chocolate chips (see
   page 24), chopped

OPTIONAL:
coconut whipped cream (see page
   256), toasted shredded coconut and
   chocolate shavings,  to serve

1. Put all the ingredients into a small saucepan over a medium heat and simmer, whisking constantly, for about 5 minutes, until steaming and the chocolate has melted.

2. Serve in small glasses – it's very rich!

# PECAN, COCONUT & LEMON GRANOLA

Crunchy and crisp, this grain-free granola is filled with healthy fats from the almonds, pecans and coconut, with a touch of zesty lemon and maple syrup. I love mine served with fresh fruit or a dollop of coconut yoghurt, but you could use full-fat natural yoghurt if you're not avoiding dairy.

*makes 300g or 2 cups*

**10 MINUTES PREPARATION TIME**
**15 MINUTES COOKING TIME**

150g (1 cup) raw almonds
150g (1 cup) raw pecans
35g (½ cup) unsweetened
   desiccated coconut
2 tablespoons coconut oil
2 tablespoons maple syrup
the zest of 1 large
   unwaxed lemon
½ teaspoon vanilla extract

1. Preheat the oven to 160°C/325°F/gas 3.

2. Chop the almonds and pecans into small pieces and put them into a large bowl. Add the remaining ingredients and stir very well until combined.

3. Spread the mixture out on a lined baking tray and bake for 15 minutes, until fragrant and golden. Leave to cool completely – the granola will crisp up. Store in an airtight container for up to 2 weeks.

# VANILLA BEAN COCONUT YOGHURT

Many homemade coconut yoghurt recipes call for expensive starter cultures and equipment, but this quick, easy and probiotic-rich recipe delivers that tangy flavour and creamy texture without all the fuss. Just mix up a few ingredients and stick in the fridge for a few hours to allow the flavours to meld – it doesn't get any simpler than that! Probiotics are bacterial cultures that are absolutely fantastic for your gut health.  They may help to regulate your digestive system and can be purchased either as a powder or in capsules online and in most health food shops; make sure the brand you purchase doesn't contain any funny filler ingredients, though.

## *makes 250ml or 1 cup*

**10 MINUTES PREPARATION TIME**

1 x 400ml tin of full-fat coconut
  milk, left in the fridge for at
  least 24 hours
1 ½ teaspoons lemon juice
½ teaspoon vanilla bean powder
½ teaspoon probiotic powder
  (either bought as a powder
  or emptied out of
  probiotic capsules)
1 teaspoon maple syrup or
  raw honey
coconut flakes, to serve

1. Open the tin of coconut milk and scoop the white, creamy part at the top into a bowl. Transfer the coconut water at the bottom of the can to a bowl, store in the fridge and use later in a smoothie.

2. To your bowl of coconut cream, add the lemon juice and vanilla bean powder. Whisk well to incorporate, then stir in your probiotic powder. If you're using capsules, carefully cut them open using scissors and empty the powder from the capsules into a very small bowl. Once you've opened a few capsules, you should have about half a teaspoon of probiotic powder in total – measure out this amount and add it to the coconut cream mixture. Mix again to evenly disperse the probiotics.

3. Transfer the mixture to a large jar or airtight container, then seal and place in the fridge for at least 4 hours to allow the flavours to meld. The coconut yoghurt will keep in the fridge for up to 5 days – just stir well before using if it has separated slightly.

4. Enjoy the yoghurt with fresh fruit, a handful of my pecan, coconut & lemon granola (see page 51) or with a dollop of raspberry chia jam (see page 66). In the photo, I've used fresh blueberries, kiwi and a sprinkling of flaked almonds. You can also add the yoghurt to smoothies or stir it into homemade curries.

# PESTO SCRAMBLED EGGS WITH AVOCADO AND GARLIC-LEMON SPINACH

A simple yet very flavourful breakfast, this one-pan meal is full of protein from the eggs, which are also rich in vitamin B12. The avocado adds plenty of healthier fats, while the spinach is rich in vitamin K. It's a great and delicious way to start the day!

*serves 2*

15 MINUTES PREPARATION TIME

1 teaspoon coconut oil
2 medium eggs
a pinch of fine sea salt and freshly ground black pepper
a very large handful of baby spinach
¼ teaspoon garlic powder
a squeeze of lemon juice
1 tablespoon homemade pesto (see page 248)
1 avocado, sliced

1. Heat the coconut oil in a frying pan over a medium heat. In a small bowl, beat the eggs with the sea salt and black pepper.

2. Add the baby spinach to the frying pan and sauté using a spatula for 1 to 2 minutes, until it wilts. Sprinkle the garlic powder over the spinach, then squeeze a few drops of lemon juice over it as well.

3. Move the spinach to the side of the pan, then add the beaten eggs and scramble with a spatula. Once scrambled, dollop the pesto on top of the eggs. Transfer the scrambled eggs and spinach to a plate and serve alongside the sliced avocado.

# CARROT, COCONUT & PINEAPPLE MUFFINS WITH WALNUT STREUSEL

These tropical muffins are a delicious grab-and-go option. Lightly spiced with cinnamon, nutmeg and a little ginger, with a crumbly streusel topping, they're filled with healthy fats from the eggs, ground almonds and coconut to keep you going for hours. You can also bake this as a loaf in a small loaf tin or as a cake in a 20cm round cake tin instead – just increase the baking time to 45 minutes and be sure to grease the tin with a little coconut oil before lining with parchment paper.

*makes* 16

10 MINUTES PREPARATION TIME
30 MINUTES COOKING TIME

FOR THE MUFFINS:
3 medium eggs
250g (2½ cups) ground almonds
1 tablespoon coconut flour
1 teaspoon ground cinnamon
¼ teaspoon ground nutmeg
¼ teaspoon ground ginger
½ teaspoon bicarbonate of soda
105g (¾ cup) coconut sugar or
    unrefined brown sugar
2 tablespoons coconut
    oil, melted
30g (¼ cup) shredded coconut
40g (¼ cup) sulphite-free dried
    pineapple, cut into small chunks
40g (¼ cup) raisins
2 large carrots, grated

FOR THE WALNUT STREUSEL:
80g (½ cup) walnuts
80g (½ cup) ground almonds
2 tablespoons coconut sugar or
    unrefined brown sugar
2 tablespoons coconut oil
1 teaspoon ground cinnamon

1. Preheat the oven to 160°C/325°F/gas 3 and line a muffin or cupcake tray with parchment paper liners.

2. To make the muffins, put the eggs, both flours, spices, bicarbonate of soda, sugar and coconut oil into a bowl and stir very well to form a smooth batter. Stir in the remaining ingredients and mix well to disperse. Evenly divide the batter between 16 paper liners.

3. To make the walnut streusel, chop the walnuts very finely, then put them into a bowl along with the rest of the streusel ingredients. Mix very well to combine, then divide between the batter-filled paper liners.

4. Bake for 30 to 35 minutes, until the muffins are golden and a toothpick inserted into the centre comes out clean. Leave to cool for 15 minutes before enjoying, or cool completely before transferring to an airtight container and freezing for up to 2 months – this way, you can pull one or two out as and when you need to.

# DATE AND ALMOND GRANOLA BARS

These are a great on-the-go breakfast – while they do have a bit of sugar from the maple syrup and dates, they've also got lots of healthy fats and protein so munching on one of these before leaving the house is a much better option than skipping breakfast. You can even crumble one over a bowl of nut milk or coconut yoghurt if you'd like!

*makes 12*

15 MINUTES PREPARATION TIME
20 MINUTES COOKING TIME

¼ cup (60ml) coconut oil
¼ cup (60ml) almond butter
¼ cup (60ml) maple syrup
½ tsp vanilla bean powder
2 cups (200g) whole raw almonds
1 cup (80g) unsweetened
   dessicated coconut
6 soft, squishy dates, pitted

1. Preheat the oven to 180C/350F/gas 4.

2. In a small saucepan over medium heat, combine the coconut oil, almond butter, maple syrup and vanilla until warmed through, stirring constantly. Try not to eat it all!

3. In a food processor, blitz together the almonds, dates and shredded coconut until you have pieces the size of breadcrumbs. Transfer to a large bowl, then pour in the liquid mixture and use a spoon or spatula to stir thoroughly to combine.

4. Grab your lined tin and press the mixture into it very firmly. Bake for 20 minutes, until golden brown, then remove from the oven and leave to cool completely before cutting into 20 small pieces. Store in an airtight container in the fridge for up to a week or the freezer for up to 3 months. Enjoy!

# ASPARAGUS & TOMATO FRITTATA SLICE

I absolutely adore frittatas – they're easy to make, brilliant to transport and delicious hot or cold, which makes them a great breakfast or lunch option. Feel free to experiment with the vegetables you add – broccoli, mushrooms and courgettes are fabulous as well as the ones I've listed here. You can also add a sprinkle of chopped fresh herbs to the beaten eggs, or make the recipe into muffins instead by using a muffin tray and reducing the baking time to about 15 minutes.

*serves 4*

**15 MINUTES PREPARATION TIME**
**25 MINUTES COOKING TIME**

6 eggs
½ teaspoon fine sea salt
¼ teaspoon freshly ground
  black pepper
100g (about 5 stalks) asparagus
1 tablespoon olive oil
2 shallots, diced
1 carrot, grated
1 red pepper, diced
a handful of baby spinach
a handful of cherry tomatoes, halved

**1.** Preheat the oven to 180°C/350°F/gas 4 and grease a small rectangular baking tin with a little oil.

**2.** In a medium bowl, beat the eggs, sea salt and black pepper well, then set aside.

**3.** Cut the bottom couple of centimetres off the asparagus, then slice into 2½cm long pieces.

**4.** Heat the olive oil in a frying pan over a medium heat, then add the shallots, grated carrot and red pepper. Sauté for 5 minutes, until tender, then add the asparagus pieces and the spinach and sauté for another few minutes.

**5.** Transfer the vegetables to the greased baking tin and top with the halved cherry tomatoes. Pour the beaten eggs over this mixture and pop it into the oven for 25 minutes, until puffed, golden and set in the middle.

**6.** Slice into pieces and serve hot alongside a salad for a delicious meal, or let the slices cool to room temperature and store in an airtight container in the fridge for up to 4 days, to enjoy later.

# OVERNIGHT BANANA ORANGE CHIA PUDDING

Chia seed pudding is a brilliant way to start your morning – chia seeds are very rich in nutrients, full of fibre and they plump up overnight to create a chunky breakfast pudding. If you don't like their texture and would rather have a creamy pudding, blend in a high-speed blender for a few minutes after it has set. You can also try out half a cup of berries, peaches or kiwi instead of the banana.

*serves* 1

**10 MINUTES PREPARATION TIME**

1 ripe banana
125ml (½ cup) homemade almond milk (see page 40)
zest and juice of ½ an orange
¼ teaspoon vanilla bean powder
3 tablespoons chia seeds

**OPTIONAL:**
a drizzle of raw honey or pure maple syrup

1. Blend together the banana, almond milk, orange zest, orange juice and vanilla bean powder until smooth in a blender or using a hand-held blender.

2. Add the chia seeds to the mixture and stir well with a spoon to disperse. Transfer the mixture to a screwtop jar, pop the lid on and leave in the fridge overnight or for at least 6 hours before enjoying. Taste and sweeten lightly with raw honey or maple syrup if required. If the texture is very thick, you can also add a little more almond milk and mix to loosen it up.

# EGG, BACON, MUSHROOM & CHIVE CUPS

A breakfast of eggs and bacon has certainly acquired a bad reputation over the last few years, but properly sourced eggs are in fact nutritional powerhouses full of amino acids and plenty of vitamin B12, while nitrate-free bacon is high in choline, which aids brain health and contains lots of protein. Fry your eggs and bacon in cold-pressed oils or coconut oil and enjoy plenty of vegetables on the side. These 'cups' are a very convenient and quick method of cooking bacon and eggs – they're also perfect for serving lots of people, as there's much less clean-up! If you're not a fan of mushrooms or would like to try something else, you can pop a slice of tomato on top of the bacon instead and skip the sautéing step.

## makes 6

**15 MINUTES PREPARATION TIME**
**20 MINUTES COOKING TIME**

coconut oil
6 slices of nitrate-free back bacon
2 big handfuls of sliced mushrooms
1 tablespoon chopped fresh chives
fine sea salt and freshly ground
    black pepper
6 eggs

1. Preheat your oven to 180°C/350°F/gas 4.

2. Grab a large 6-hole muffin tray and grease it thoroughly with coconut oil. Line each hole with one slice of bacon, pressing it around the sides and the bottom of the hole and making sure to cover every bit.

3. Heat a large frying pan with a little coconut oil over a medium heat. Add the sliced mushrooms, chopped chives and a pinch of sea salt and sauté for 5 to 6 minutes, until the mushrooms are cooked through. Divide the mushroom and chive mixture evenly between the muffin cups.

4. Crack an egg into each hole, sprinkle a little sea salt and black pepper over each cup and bake for 18 to 20 minutes, until the bacon is done but the egg yolks are still runny – you can cook them for a little longer if you'd prefer the eggs fully cooked.

5. Run a knife along the edge of each muffin hole to loosen the egg and bacon cups, then gently ease them out. Serve hot, with a green leafy salad.

# LEMON POPPYSEED SCONES WITH RASPBERRY CHIA JAM

Golden and zesty, these lemon poppyseed scones are full of great ingredients. They're definitely best generously slathered with coconut whipped cream and this raspberry chia jam! The jam is incredibly quick and easy and the chia seeds thicken it up, with a touch of natural sweetness from the maple syrup. If you're not a fan of coconut, just serve the scones with plenty of jam, or if you'd like to experiment with other flavours in the scones, add a handful of fresh berries or chopped dried fruit.

*makes* 10

**15 MINUTES PREPARATION TIME**
**20 MINUTES COOKING TIME**

**FOR THE SCONES:**
175g (1¾ cups) ground almonds
75g (½ cup + 2 tablespoons)
   coconut flour
1 tablespoon poppy seeds
1 teaspoon bicarbonate of soda
125ml (½ cup) coconut oil, melted
125ml (½ cup) maple syrup
the zest and juice of 2
   unwaxed lemons
125ml (½ cup) full-fat tinned
   coconut milk
3 eggs

**FOR THE RASPBERRY CHIA JAM:**
150g raspberries (fresh or frozen
   and defrosted)
1 tablespoon chia seeds
1 tablespoon hot water
2 tablespoons maple syrup

1. Preheat the oven to 180°C/350°F/gas 4. Line a muffin tray with parchment paper liners.

2. Start off by making the raspberry chia jam – just put everything into the blender and whizz until well combined. Transfer to a screwtop jar and leave to set in the fridge for at least 30 minutes.

3. To make the scones, whisk together the ground almonds, coconut flour, poppy seeds, bicarbonate of soda and lemon zest in a large bowl.

4. In a small bowl, whisk the coconut oil, maple syrup, lemon juice, coconut milk and eggs. Add this to the dry ingredients and mix to form a batter. Use an ice-cream scoop or a big spoon to fill the muffin liners about two-thirds full with batter, until all the batter is used up.

5. Bake the scones for 20 minutes, until golden. Serve warm or at room temperature, with a big dollop of coconut whipped cream (see page 256) and a smattering of raspberry chia jam!

6. The jam will keep in a sealed jar in the fridge for up to a week, and any leftover scones will keep for up to 5 days in an airtight container at room temperature.

# BREAKFAST BURRITO WRAPS

Warm, hearty and with plenty of flavour, these burrito wraps are a fantastic option if you're craving a tortilla or you're cooking for a crowd – you can double or triple the tortilla recipe and the red pepper mixture, then set out bowls of toppings such as sliced jalapeños, diced avocado, chopped tomato, black olives and chopped coriander so that everyone can add their own twist!

## makes 2

**20 MINUTES PREPARATION TIME**

a little coconut oil
1 medium red pepper, sliced
1 clove of garlic, chopped
1 shallot, diced
2 eggs, beaten well
a pinch of fine sea salt and freshly
  ground black pepper
¼ teaspoon chilli powder
  teaspoon paprika
a few cherry tomatoes, chopped
½ an avocado, diced
2 homemade tortilla wraps
  (see page 254)

**OPTIONAL TOPPINGS:**
black olives, chopped coriander,
  sliced jalapeños

1. Preheat the oven to 200°C/400°F/gas 6.

2. Melt a little coconut oil in a frying pan over a medium heat, then toss in the sliced red pepper, chopped garlic and diced shallot. Sauté for about 2 minutes, until the shallots are starting to colour, then reduce the heat to low and cook for a further 5 minutes, until the red pepper has softened. Add your beaten eggs, a pinch of sea salt and black pepper, the chilli powder and the paprika. Scramble the eggs with the red pepper mixture, then divide this mixture between the 2 tortilla wraps, lining it up with the centre of the wraps for easy rolling.

3. Divide the tomatoes and diced avocado between the two wraps, then roll them up. Wrap tightly with foil and place in the preheated oven for 5 minutes. Enjoy hot, with a scattering of fresh coriander!

# FLUFFY PANCAKE STACK FOR ONE

This recipe has taken me a long while to perfect, but I've finally arrived at fluffy, tall pancake perfection! This recipe makes a stack of pancakes for one, and is perfect for a quick breakfast. The pancakes contain fibre-rich coconut flour along with coconut oil and an egg, to provide lots of nourishment to start your day. If you like, you can experiment with adding ingredients to the batter before cooking the pancakes as well – try lemon zest and a handful of fresh blueberries. If you're really short on time in the morning, you can even mix up the dry ingredients in a bowl the night before and just add the coconut oil, almond milk and egg the next day!

*serves 1*

**5 MINUTES PREPARATION TIME**

1 ½ tablespoons arrowroot
1 ½ tablespoons coconut flour
½ teaspoon baking powder
2 teaspoons coconut sugar or
  unrefined brown sugar
2 teaspoons coconut oil
3 tablespoons almond milk
1 egg

1. In a small bowl, whisk together the arrowroot, coconut flour, baking powder and coconut sugar until combined. Add the coconut oil, almond milk and egg, then beat to form a smooth mixture.

2. Heat a large frying pan over a low-medium heat and add a little coconut oil.

3. Beat the pancake batter again, then spoon the mixture into the pan to form 4 small pancakes, each about 5cm in diameter.

4. Cook for 3 to 4 minutes, until golden on the bottom, then flip each pancake and cook for another 3 minutes or so until done.

5. Serve immediately with toppings – you could try fresh fruit, a little maple syrup, nut butter, raspberry chia jam (see page 66) or even chocolate chips.

*tip*

This recipe makes the perfect amount for one, but to make enough to feed four hungry friends or family members, use 6 tablespoons of arrowroot, 6 tablespoons of coconut flour, 2 teaspoons of baking powder, 2 tablespoons each of coconut sugar and coconut oil, 175ml (3/4 cup) of almond milk and 5 eggs.

# HAZELNUT CHOCOLATE CHIP WAFFLES

The combination of hazelnuts and chocolate, especially at breakfast, really is an indulgent one. I love making these waffles for special occasions, as they're easy to make in advance. If you're having trouble finding roasted ground hazelnuts (many supermarkets stock them) or have run out, you can substitute ground almonds, and feel free to use sunflower seed flour (see page 23) instead for a nut-free version, although the use of baking powder in the recipe will react with the sunflower seeds and turn the waffles green – perfect for a St Patrick's day breakfast! For a twist, leave out the chocolate chips or chopped chocolate and use a handful of fresh blueberries instead.

*serves 4*

**15 MINUTES PREPARATION TIME**

150g (1½ cups) roasted
  ground hazelnuts
110g (¾ cup) arrowroot
35g (¼ cup) coconut sugar or
  unrefined brown sugar
½ teaspoon vanilla bean powder
2 teaspoons baking powder
2 tablespoons coconut oil
175ml (¾ cup) almond milk
50g high-quality chopped dark
  chocolate or dark chocolate
  chips (see page 24)

**OPTIONAL:**
a tablespoon of hazelnut butter,
  to serve

1. Put the ground hazelnuts, arrowroot, coconut sugar, vanilla bean powder and baking powder into a food processor and whizz for about 2 minutes, until very fine. Add the coconut oil and almond milk, then whizz for another minute or so until fully combined. Remove the blade of the food processor and stir in the chopped chocolate or chocolate chips with a spoon until dispersed.

2. Turn your waffle maker on and rub it with a little coconut oil on a piece of kitchen paper to prevent the waffles sticking. Once hot, put a scoop of batter into the waffle maker and cook according to the manufacturer's instructions until the waffles are golden and crisp.

3. Remove from the waffle maker and repeat until all the batter is used up. Serve piping hot, with a drizzle of hazelnut butter if you wish.

4. If you're making them to eat later, let the waffles cool completely and transfer them to an airtight container or a resealable bag before popping them into the freezer. To defrost, throw them into a 200°C/400°F/gas 6 oven for 5 to 8 minutes until nice and hot, then enjoy.

# SOUPS, SIDES & GREEN STUFF

I know these are often shoved to the side with an 'Ugh, do I have to eat that?' – but if that sounds familiar, you're missing out! Although salads, soups and veg have a reputation for being bland and boring, they're anything but. Chock-full of nutrients, colour and flavour, these recipes range from salads you can throw together in two minutes to nourishing soups for when you're craving comfort food, and if you're feeling uninspired, take a look at the salad guide for a few new ideas to shake up your salad game!

# BASIC STOCK & HOMEMADE STOCK CUBES

Flavourful, rich stocks are a delicious and nutritious addition to soups and stews. If made with chicken and beef bones, make sure you're using well-sourced bones from high-welfare meat. You can source these from your local butcher (where they're often given away for free!) or you can use the leftover bones from a roast. That said, nobody has the time to simmer up a fresh batch of broth to enjoy every day or even a few times a week – although it's easy to chuck everything into a pot, the stock needs to simmer for a few hours, which can be difficult to fit into a busy schedule. Homemade stock cubes to the rescue! Made from just stock, the recipe does require you to watch the mixture quite carefully in the last half an hour of cooking, but it will leave you with a big batch of stock cubes which will last you a while in the freezer. The convenience of having them tucked away whenever I need stock is well worth the extra hour to me!

### makes 2 litres or 8 cups

**15 MINUTES PREPARATION TIME**
**10 HOURS COOKING TIME**

500g well-sourced bones (if making beef or chicken-based stock only)
2½ litres (10 cups) water
2 leeks, sliced
2 carrots, sliced
5 stalk of celery, sliced
3 shallots, diced
1 bay leaf
a few sprigs of fresh parsley
1 teaspoon whole black peppercorns
½ teaspoon coarse salt

1. To make beef/chicken-based stock: if using bones which have not been previously roasted (like they would be if you're using the leftover carcass from a roast chicken, for example), pop them on a baking tray and roast for 30 minutes at 180°C/350°F/gas 4. Transfer to a large pot over a high heat, then add the water, vegetables, herbs and spices, and bring to the boil. Once it has reached a vigorous boil, reduce the heat to low and let the stock simmer for 2 to 3 hours. Remove from the heat and allow to cool slightly, then strain through a sieve and discard all the bones and vegetables. When cool, transfer the stock to a glass jar and leave sealed in the fridge overnight. The next day, use a spoon to scrape off the layer of fat which will gather at the top of the stock, then leave it sealed in the fridge for up to 5 days, or freeze for later use. You can also turn the stock into homemade stock cubes at this point – see page 78.

2. To make vegetable stock: chop up your veggies, then heat 1 tablespoon of olive oil in a large pot over a medium heat. Add the leeks, carrots, celery and shallots ➤

and sauté for 2 to 3 minutes, until fragrant, then add the herbs and spices and the water. Bring to the boil, then turn the heat to low and simmer for 2 hours. Strain through a sieve, discard the solids, then transfer to a glass jar when cool and keep sealed in the fridge for up to 5 days, or turn into homemade stock cubes!

3. To make homemade stock cubes: put 2 litres (8 cups) (the amount both recipes above will yield) of stock into a medium pot and set over a high heat. Boil uncovered for about half an hour, until the mixture is half its original volume, then reduce the heat to low and simmer for another half an hour or so, until the stock is thick and syrupy and any bubbling has subsided. You'll want to watch it closely and stir well with a spoon every few minutes for the last half hour, as it could burn if left for too long or at too high a heat. Once the mixture is thick and is not bubbling up as much, immediately transfer it to a small square or rectangular container. Let it cool overnight in the fridge, where it will set, then cut into 8 homemade stock cubes. Pop the cubes into a resealable bag and place in the freezer, where they will keep for up to a year. Each stock cube can be dissolved in 250ml (1 cup) of boiling water to make the equivalent of 250ml (1 cup) of stock.

# CREAM OF TOMATO SOUP

Forget the tins – this tomato soup is rich, creamy and very easy to make as well. My family loves it served with seed-sprinkled garlic & oregano crackers (see page 253). It's best eaten fresh and hot, as the flavour deteriorates when it's left in the fridge for too long!

*serves 6*

**10 MINUTES PREPARATION TIME**
**30 MINUTES COOKING TIME**

1 tablespoon extra virgin olive oil
3 medium shallots, chopped
2 cloves of garlic, thinly sliced
1 large leek, sliced
2 small carrots, roughly chopped
2 teaspoons fine sea salt
2 x 400g tins of chopped tomatoes
600ml (2½ cups) homemade beef or
   vegetable stock, or 2 homemade
   stock cubes (see pages 76–79)
   dissolved in 600ml (2½ cups)
   boiling water
300ml (1¼ cups) almond milk

1. Heat the olive oil in a large saucepan over a medium heat. Add the shallots, garlic, leek and carrots, stir well, turn the heat to low, then cover the pan with a lid and cook for 7 to 8 minutes.

2. Add the sea salt, tomatoes and stock to the pan, then increase the heat and bring the mixture to a boil before reducing the heat a little and letting the soup simmer, covered with a lid, for 20 minutes.

3. Remove the pan from the heat and blend the soup with a stick blender. Add the almond milk and blend again to incorporate. Serve hot, straight away.

# CUMIN, CARROT & ROASTED BUTTERNUT SQUASH BISQUE

Hearty and warming, this beta-carotene-packed butternut squash soup is taken up a notch thanks to the roasting and the addition of cumin, chilli flakes and carrots. It's quite spicy, so reduce the chilli if you're looking for a more mellow soup! The flavour pairs perfectly with my seed-sprinkled garlic & oregano crackers (see page 253), and the soup is also great with leftover shredded chicken for a protein boost.

*serves 4*

**10 MINUTES PREPARATION TIME**
**1 HOUR COOKING TIME**

1 medium butternut squash, halved and deseeded
2 tablespoons extra virgin olive oil
3 shallots, diced
2 cloves of garlic, chopped
1 teaspoon ground cumin
¼ teaspoon chilli flakes
2 large carrots, peeled and finely diced
a pinch of fine sea salt and freshly ground black pepper
1 litre (4 cups) homemade vegetable or chicken stock or 4 homemade stock cubes (see pages 76–79) dissolved in 1 litre (4 cups) boiling water

1. Preheat the oven to 200°C/400°F/gas 6. Pop your butternut squash halves on a baking tray and drizzle with 1 tablespoon of the oil, then place in the oven and roast for about 45 minutes, until the squash flesh is tender. Once cooked, set aside.

2. Heat the remaining olive oil in a saucepan over a medium heat, then add the shallots, garlic, cumin and chilli flakes. Sauté for 3 to 4 minutes, then add the carrots and a pinch of sea salt and black pepper and sauté for another minute or two.

3. Use a spoon to scoop out the soft roasted butternut squash flesh and add it to the saucepan, then pour over the stock and bring to a simmer. Simmer for about 10 minutes, until the carrots are soft, then use an immersion blender to blitz to a smooth, creamy bisque.

4. Serve immediately, with a sprinkle of spicy roasted seeds (see page 15) and a scattering of chopped fresh coriander or thinly sliced red chilli.

*Tip*

Replace half the butternut squash with pumpkin during the autumn months for a seasonal twist!

# ASPARAGUS SOUP WITH CRISPY SHALLOTS

This creamy soup tastes best when you use fresh, seasonal asparagus, as the simplicity of the other ingredients really allows its flavour to shine. Adding the cayenne and the lemon juice at the very end is key to brightening the soup up and also provides some vitamin C. You can make the crispy shallots up to 2 hours ahead of time, and the soup will keep in a sealed container in the fridge for up to 2 days, although you'll want to reheat it and squeeze in a bit more lemon juice before serving.

*serves 2*

**10 MINUTES PREPARATION TIME**
**30 MINUTES COOKING TIME**

FOR THE ASPARAGUS SOUP:
500g fresh asparagus
1 tablespoon olive oil
2 shallots, chopped
1 leek, sliced
fine sea salt and freshly ground
   black pepper, to taste
500ml (2 cups) fresh chicken stock,
   or 2 homemade stock cubes (see
   pages 76–79) dissolved in 500ml
   (2 cups) boiling water
60ml (½ cup) almond milk
a good squeeze of lime juice
   (about 2 teaspoons)
a pinch of cayenne pepper

FOR THE CRISPY SHALLOTS:
5 shallots
2 tablespoons coconut oil
½ teaspoon fine sea salt

1. Cut a couple of centimetres of the woody bottoms off the asparagus and discard, then slice the asparagus into 1cm pieces.

2. Heat the olive oil in a pot over a medium heat, then add the chopped shallots and sauté for about a minute. Add the asparagus pieces, leeks and a pinch of sea salt and black pepper, then cook for 5 minutes, stirring often. Pour in your stock, cover the pot and simmer for about 10 to 15 minutes, until the asparagus stalks are completely soft.

3. Meanwhile, make the crispy shallots. Slice them as thinly as you can, then heat about 2 tablespoons of oil – I really like to use a 'cuisine' coconut oil here (see page 22) so as not to interfere with the shallot flavour – in a frying pan over a medium heat. Once hot, add your thinly sliced shallots and sea salt and sauté, stirring constantly, for about 10 minutes, until they're golden brown and crispy. Once ready, quickly remove them from the oil and transfer them to a plate lined with kitchen paper to crisp them up. Let them cool for 2 or 3 minutes, taste, sprinkle with a little more sea salt if necessary, then set aside while you finish the soup.

4. Remove the soup from the heat, add the almond milk and blend with a hand-held blender until completely smooth, then bring it back to the boil. Stir in your lime juice and cayenne pepper and serve immediately, with a scattering of crispy shallots, flaked almonds and some chopped chives.

# NOURISHING CHICKEN COURGETTE NOODLE SOUP

This is chicken 'noodle' soup reinvented – I've packed highly nutritious courgette noodles and lots of vegetables into a hearty chicken stock to create a warming, nourishing meal. You can use a spiralizer to turn the courgettes into 'noodles' if you have one, or use this much cheaper method instead: grab a vegetable peeler, peel thick vertical strips of the courgette, then stack the slices up and use a sharp knife to cut the slices into thin, long vertical strips. If you have some leftover cooked chicken, chuck that in instead of the chicken thighs, and try to use fresh herbs here whenever possible, as they add so much more flavour; if you're out of them, though, just use half a teaspoon of the dried variety instead.

*serves 4*

**10 MINUTES PREPARATION TIME**
**20 MINUTES COOKING TIME**

a splash of coconut oil
4 shallots, diced
1 stalk of celery, diced
1 large carrot, sliced
2 cloves of garlic, chopped
a pinch of fine sea salt, freshly ground
  black pepper and chilli flakes
1 teaspoon each of chopped fresh
  thyme, parsley and oregano
1½ litres (6 cups) homemade
  chicken stock, or 6 homemade
  stock cubes (see pages
  76–79) dissolved in 1½ litres
  (6 cups) boiling water
4 skinless, boneless chicken thighs
  (or 2 skinless, boneless chicken
  breast fillets)
4 courgettes
a small handful of fresh parsley,
  chopped, to garnish

1. Heat the coconut oil in a large pot over a medium heat and add the shallots, celery, carrot, garlic, seasoning and fresh herbs. Sauté for 2 to 3 minutes, until fragrant and the shallots are beginning to turn translucent.

2. Add the chicken stock and the chicken and bring to the boil, then simmer for about 20 minutes.

3. Meanwhile, turn your courgettes into noodles using either a spiralizer or the method described above, and set aside.

4. Once the chicken is cooked, remove it from the soup and either shred into bits using two forks or chop into chunks. Return the shredded or chopped chicken and the courgette noodles to the soup and cook for 5 minutes, until the courgette noodles are just tender.

5. Serve immediately, with a sprinkle of chopped parsley. Leftovers keep well in a sealed container in the fridge for up to 2 days, or frozen for up to a month.

# SPICY THAI RED CURRY SOUP

You can't go wrong with a fragrant, spicy oriental soup, and this is my absolute favourite. With plenty of garlic, ginger and lemongrass for a kick along with a good dollop of Thai red curry paste, which is made with red chilli, lemongrass and kaffir lime for a beautiful colour and authentic taste, it's sure to warm you up and wake up your tastebuds! I've added baby spinach and red pepper for some extra nutrition and stunning colours, but you can use seasonal vegetables like green beans, mushrooms or courgettes instead, if you like.

*serves 4*

**10 MINUTES PREPARATION TIME**
**20 MINUTES COOKING TIME**

1 stalk of lemongrass, about 8cm
   in length
1 tablespoon coconut oil
2 cloves of garlic, chopped
a 2½cm piece of fresh ginger,
   peeled and chopped
1 shallot, diced
3–5 teaspoons Thai red curry paste
   (preferably choose a brand that's
   organic and doesn't contain refined
   sugars or any unnecessary additives
   or sulphites, and adjust the spiciness
   to taste – 3 teaspoons is more than
   enough for me, but taste as you go
   and add more if needed!)
2 spring onions, sliced
the juice and zest of ½ a lime
a handful of fresh coriander,
   finely chopped
1 red pepper, deseeded and sliced
1 x 400ml tin of full-fat coconut milk
1 very large handful of baby spinach
a pinch of fine sea salt

**OPTIONAL:**
200g raw chicken strips or peeled
   and deveined raw prawns
a small handful of coriander, chopped,
   and ½ a lime cut into wedges,
   to garnish

1. Using a large sharp knife, slice your stalk of lemongrass from top to bottom and use this cut to remove the outer layer of the stalk. Discard this outer layer, then lay the blade of your knife flat on the thickest part of the lemongrass. Carefully use the palm of your hand to smack down on the flat blade a few times until the lemongrass stalk bursts – this releases lots of flavour. Now thinly slice the stalk and set aside.

2. Heat the coconut oil in a saucepan over medium heat, then add the garlic, ginger and shallot. Sauté for 1 to 2 minutes, until fragrant and starting to soften, then add your curry paste and fry it for about a minute – mash it a bit with a spatula and stir around the pan to bring out the delicious flavour. Throw in the sliced lemongrass, sliced spring onions, lime juice and zest, chopped coriander and sliced red pepper and sauté for a further 3 to 4 minutes, until the pepper is starting to soften.

3. Add the coconut milk and give it a stir to disperse. Bring the mixture to a simmer and cook for 10 minutes. If you're using the chicken or prawns, toss those in at this stage and cook for a further 10 minutes, until they're fully cooked, then add the baby spinach at the last minute and stir for about a minute, until wilted. If you're not adding the protein source, just add the baby spinach and wilt for a minute or two.

4. Serve hot, with a garnish of chopped coriander and a wedge of lime. Store leftovers in a sealed container in the fridge for up to 2 days and reheat thoroughly before serving.

# CHILLED CUCUMBER, AVOCADO & DILL SOUP

This refreshing chilled soup is the perfect way to cool down on a sunny day. Cucumbers are very hydrating, while the healthy fats and vitamin E in the avocado is great for your skin and hair. With zingy lime and fragrant dill to spice things up, this soup will quickly become a favourite; it's incredibly easy to make ahead and is great served as a light lunch or appetizer. Try substituting fresh coriander for the dill for a twist!

*serves 2*

**10 MINUTES PREPARATION TIME**
**10 MINUTES COOKING TIME**
**+ 3 HOURS REFRIGERATING TIME**

a splash of olive oil
2 shallots, diced
250ml (1 cup) vegetable or chicken
   stock, or ½ a homemade stock
   cube (see pages 76–79) dissolved in
   250ml (1 cup) boiling water
1 large cucumber, seeded and
   chopped (I leave the peel on for the
   gorgeous colour, but peel your
   cucumber if it's not organic)
the green part of 1 spring
   onion, sliced
the juice of ½ a lime
fine sea salt and freshly ground
   black pepper, to taste
about 2 tablespoons of fresh dill,
   finely chopped
1 soft, ripe avocado, pitted, peeled
   and chopped

1. Heat a saucepan over a medium heat and add the olive oil. Add the shallots and sauté for 2 to 3 minutes, until fragrant and soft, then add the stock, cucumber, spring onion, lime juice and a pinch of sea salt and black pepper. Bring to a simmer, cover the pan with a lid and cook for about 10 minutes, until the cucumber is soft.

2. Remove from the heat, add the fresh dill and avocado and either blend with a hand-held blender or transfer the mixture to a food processor/blender and whizz until smooth and creamy. Taste, adjust the seasoning if necessary by adding some sea salt or a squeeze of lime juice, then pop it into the fridge for at least 3 hours, until completely chilled. Serve cold, with a scattering of spring onions, a little fresh dill and some finely chopped cucumber or avocado if you wish.

# THE ULTIMATE SALAD GUIDE

Creating a tasty, nutritious salad isn't difficult as long as you keep it varied and include plenty of delicious greens, veggies, toppings, dressings and flavour boosters! Here's how I like to create a great plate of greens.

## 1 choose some leaves (a few very large handfuls)

I tend to use a mixture of these for the best flavour; I use either a combination I've created myself or a pre-bagged salad mix for convenience.

- rocket
- baby spinach
- watercress
- romaine or cos lettuce, torn into bite-size pieces
- baby gem lettuce leaves

## 2 add some colourful veggies (a handful of each)

I find that a variety of bright, crunchy vegetables is key to creating a delicious salad. Try to use two or three of the below so that you have all sorts of textures, flavours and colours in order to make your salad more exciting.

- cherry tomatoes
- red peppers
- radishes
- cucumber
- avocado – squeeze a little lime juice on top to prevent browning
- shredded carrot
- grated raw or cooked beetroot

## 3 throw in some toppings (a handful)

These are my favourite things to scatter on top of salads for lots of flavour!

- sliced olives
- roasted spicy seeds (see page 15)
- chopped nuts
- pieces of my seeded crackers (see page 253)
- sliced hard-boiled eggs
- roasted wild salmon or line-caught tinned tuna
- leftover sliced or shredded chicken

## 4 finish it off with some flavour boosters (a small handful)

Just a small handful or spoonful of these can add so much to your salad. From fresh herbs to seasonal fruit, there's no way your salad will be boring with a few of these stirred in!

- plenty of fresh herbs – I love basil, parsley, chives and spring onions
- a spoonful of pesto (see page 248)
- a bit of seasonal fruit – berries, pears, apples, oranges and pomegranate seeds are all wonderful
- a squeeze of lime juice
- a sprinkling of sesame seeds

# CUCUMBER RIBBON, RADISH, SPRING ONION & SUGAR SNAP SALAD

Super green and very refreshing, this is one of my favourite summer salads to throw together quickly. If you haven't got a spiralizer, you can use a vegetable peeler to peel long strips of cucumber and use those instead, and replace the radishes with a thinly sliced red pepper if you're not a fan of them. The dressing can be made in advance, and the radishes, spring onions and sugar snaps can be prepped a few hours ahead as well, but you should make the cucumber ribbons and assemble the salad at the very last minute, right before serving, to prevent the salad from going soggy. Top with cashews that you've roasted in some coconut oil and fine sea salt for 10 minutes at 180°C/350°F/gas 4 for an extra bit of crunch and some of protein if you wish!

*serves 2*

**15 MINUTES PREPARATION TIME**

**FOR THE SALAD:**
4 medium radishes, thinly sliced
2 big handfuls of sugar snap peas, roughly chopped
2 spring onions, thinly sliced (white and green parts)
1 large cucumber, spiralized or prepared as described above
a handful of fresh chives, sliced

**FOR THE DRESSING:**
2 tablespoons extra virgin olive oil
the juice of ½ a lemon
a big handful of fresh parsley
a pinch of fine sea salt and freshly ground black pepper

1. To make the dressing, put the ingredients into a blender or food processor (or use a hand-held blender) and blitz for about a minute, until completely smooth. It'll keep for up to a day in a sealed jar in the fridge.

2. Slice the radishes, roughly chop the sugar snap peas and slice the spring onions, then pop them into a bowl. You can cover the bowl and keep it in the fridge for a few hours before serving if you like.

3. Right before serving, make the cucumber ribbons, pat them dry using kitchen paper and add them to the bowl with the other veg and the chives. Pour over all the dressing and toss very well until completely combined. Serve immediately.

# CABBAGE, CARROT & APPLE SHRED WITH THAI ALMOND BUTTER DRESSING

This colourful cabbage shred is absolutely packed with nutrients and flavour. The crunch and the slight sweetness of the carrots and apples goes perfectly with the creamy Thai-inspired almond butter dressing, which contains anti-inflammatory apple cider vinegar and plenty of zingy lime juice.

*serves 4 as a side dish*

**15 MINUTES PREPARATION TIME**

**FOR THE CABBAGE SHRED:**
½ a small white cabbage
4 carrots, peeled
2 apples, cored
a handful of homemade roasted & sea salted cashews (see page 15), crushed

**FOR THE THAI ALMOND BUTTER DRESSING:**
½ a clove of garlic, finely chopped
2 tablespoons roasted almond butter
1 tablespoon fresh lime juice
2 tablespoons hot water
1 tablespoon coconut aminos (see page 23) or gluten-free tamari
1 teaspoon maple syrup
1 teaspoon apple cider vinegar
1 spring onion, thinly sliced

1. Slice the bottom off the cabbage, then quarter it lengthways. Use a sharp knife to cut a triangular piece from the bottom of each wedge in order to remove the cabbage's tough core.

2. Set a grating blade in your food processor and use it to grate the carrots, apples, and cored white cabbage wedges, or simply grate them all with a box grater. Transfer the shredded veg to a large bowl and mix to combine.

3. To make the dressing, stir all the ingredients together in a small bowl until fully combined. If you're serving the salad right away, add the dressing to the shredded veg and toss thoroughly, then serve immediately with a scattering of the crushed cashews. Otherwise, keep the salad and dressing separate until just before serving to prevent it from going soggy.

# TOMATO, MINT & PARSLEY
# CHOPPED SALAD

Super quick yet ridiculously flavourful, this colourful salad got its name because it literally only requires a chopping board along with a handful of veg and a smattering of fresh herbs. Finished off with a simple olive oil and lemon juice dressing to bring out the flavour of the ingredients, it's quick, easy and perfect for a last-minute side dish; serve with grilled or sautéed lemon-marinated chicken (see page 39) for a light, bright summery meal.

*serves 4 as a side dish*

**10 MINUTES PREPARATION TIME**

1 tablespoon extra virgin olive oil
1 tablespoon lemon juice
a pinch each of fine sea salt and
   freshly ground black pepper
1 green pepper, deseeded and sliced
350g cherry tomatoes, halved
½ a red onion, finely chopped
a very big handful of fresh parsley,
   roughly chopped
a small handful of fresh
   mint, chopped

1. In a small bowl, whisk together the olive oil, lemon juice, sea salt and black pepper. Put the sliced green pepper, halved cherry tomatoes, chopped red onion and chopped herbs into a medium bowl and drizzle over the dressing.

2. Toss gently to combine and serve immediately.

# CUCUMBER RED ONION SALAD

Tangy and refreshing, the combination of crisp, cool cucumber with sharp red onion makes for a delicious salad. Don't skip the resting – it really allows the flavours to blend.

*serves 4 as a side*

10 MINUTES PREPARATION TIME

1 tablespoon white wine vinegar
a pinch of fine sea salt
1 large cucumber, quartered and thinly sliced
½ a red onion, thinly sliced
2 spring onions, thinly sliced

1. Put all the ingredients into a large bowl and toss to combine.

2. Let the salad sit at room temperature for about 15 minutes to allow the flavours to meld before serving.

# GARLICKY GREEN BEANS WITH CHERRY TOMATOES & BALSAMIC

Green beans are blanched in hot water and plunged into an ice bath before being sautéed with garlic, cherry tomatoes and balsamic in this quick, flavourful side dish. Use the freshest beans you can find for the best flavour – they're in season throughout the summer. The balsamic vinegar adds a whole new tangy dimension, but feel free to leave it out if you're not a fan. You can also halve the garlic if you wish.

*serves 4 as a side*

**10 MINUTES PREPARATION TIME**
**15 MINUTES COOKING TIME**

fine sea salt and freshly ground
   black pepper
500g green beans, tops and
   bottoms trimmed
2 tablespoons extra virgin
   olive oil
2 cloves of garlic, finely chopped
a handful of cherry
   tomatoes, halved
1 tablespoon balsamic vinegar

1. Fill a large pot with boiling water, add a generous pinch of sea salt and add the trimmed beans as soon as the water boils. Cook for 5 minutes, until the beans still have a little bite and are a beautiful bright green.

2. Meanwhile, fill a big bowl with cold water and a few handfuls of ice. Once the beans are done cooking, immediately lower them into the iced water and leave for a few minutes, until fully cooled, then drain and set aside.

3. Heat the olive oil in a saucepan over medium heat, add the garlic and sauté for a minute. Add the green beans, cherry tomatoes and a pinch of sea salt and black pepper and stir well for about 4 minutes, until the tomatoes begin to blister, then stir in the balsamic vinegar and toss to combine. Serve immediately.

# BRAISED SWEET POTATO MASH

Sweet potatoes are an incredibly nutritious vegetable rich in betacarotene, which the body converts to vitamin A. Their subtle, sweet flavour is often overpowered by strong spices or ruined by being boiled to bits. Braising the sweet potatoes in almond milk creates a creamy, beautiful and delicious mash and really allows their flavour to shine through as well as enhancing their natural sweetness.

*serves 4 as a side*

**5 MINUTES PREPARATION TIME**
**40 MINUTES COOKING TIME**

2 large sweet potatoes, peeled
a pinch of fine sea salt
165ml (2/3 cup) almond milk or
    full-fat milk
2 tablespoons coconut oil

1. Slice the sweet potatoes into ½cm thick slices. The important thing here is that they're all approximately the same thickness so that they cook evenly.

2. Put the sea salt and almond milk into a saucepan over a medium heat until it reaches a steady simmer, then add the sweet potatoes and coconut oil.

3. Cover the pan, then reduce the heat slightly to medium-low and cook, stirring every few minutes, for 30 to 40 minutes, until the sweet potato slices are very, very tender and falling apart. The braising liquid should be simmering gently throughout the cooking time, so you might need to adjust the heat a little if your almond milk isn't bubbling.

4. Once tender, remove the pan from the heat and smash with a fork for a chunky mash or use a hand-held blender for a smooth, creamy mash. Taste and adjust the seasoning if necessary. Leftovers keep well in an airtight container in the fridge for up to 2 days.

*tip*

For a spicy twist, add a teaspoon of ground cinnamon and a teaspoon of ground ginger just after mashing!

# SAUTÉED MUSHROOMS WITH GARLIC & PARSLEY

It doesn't get much easier than these quick and easy sautéd button mushrooms. Mushrooms are packed with umami flavour and riboflavin, which aids red blood cell production, and these are brilliant alongside a stir-fry with plenty of seasonal veg or piled on top of a grilled steak with a green salad. Cooking mushrooms can be quite tricky: you don't want them to steam or boil, as this leads to a bland, soggy dish – make sure you don't crowd them so the moisture can evaporate quickly.

*serves 4 as a side*

**5 MINUTES PREPARATION TIME**
**15 MINUTES COOKING TIME**

1 tablespoon extra virgin
  olive oil
500g button mushrooms,
  washed and thinly sliced
a small pinch of fine sea salt and
  freshly ground black pepper
1 clove of garlic, finely chopped
a handful of fresh
  parsley, chopped

1. Heat the oil in a large frying pan over a medium-high heat, then add the mushrooms, spreading them out in a single layer. In order for the mushrooms to caramelize and turn a lovely golden brown, you'll need to make sure that the pan is hot enough for them to quickly release any moisture. You should hear them sizzle when they hit the pan.

2. Sauté for about 2 minutes, until they start to release a little moisture, then continue to cook for another few minutes until all the liquid has evaporated and the mushrooms turn golden brown. Add the sea salt, black pepper, garlic and parsley, and toss for about a minute, until the garlic has softened, then serve.

# CUMIN & TURMERIC ROASTED CAULIFLOWER

Cauliflower definitely has a bad reputation – bland, overcooked or soggy is
the norm – but roasting brings out its best side. With crispy edges, a nutty flavour
and a slight bite, it undergoes a total transformation in the oven; a few spices,
a drizzle of oil and a dash of sea salt is all it needs.

*serves 4 as a side*

**10 MINUTES PREPARATION TIME**
**30 MINUTES COOKING TIME**

2 tablespoons extra virgin
  olive oil
½ teaspoon fine sea salt
1 teaspoon ground cumin
½ teaspoon ground turmeric
1 head of cauliflower, cored and
  cut into florets

1. Preheat the oven to 200°C/400°F/gas 6.

2. In a small bowl, combine the olive oil, sea salt, cumin and
turmeric.

3. Pop the cauliflower into a big bowl, drizzle over the
spiced oil and toss well to combine.

4. Spread the cauliflower on a lined baking tray in
a single layer.

5. Roast for 25 to 30 minutes, until golden around the
edges and the stalks of the cauliflower florets are tender
when you stab them with a sharp knife.

# EASY ROASTED VEG

This is one of my staples – it's delicious, really healthy and all you need to do is chop up some vegetables and throw them in the oven. Experiment with the flavours you like. I particularly love squash with tomatoes and peppers, and if you have any pesto (page 248) or carrot-curry sauce (page 242) on hand, drizzle some of that over right before serving for a delicious twist!

*serves 4 as a side*

**15 MINUTES PREPARATION TIME**
**45 MINUTES COOKING TIME**

1 courgette, sliced into 1cm pieces
2 carrots, peeled and sliced into
   1cm pieces
½ a butternut squash, peeled,
   deseeded and sliced into
   small chunks
1 red pepper, deseeded and cut into
   large strips
2 tomatoes, cut into quarters
1 tbsp extra virgin olive oil
a few sprigs of fresh thyme
   or rosemary
plenty of sea salt and freshly ground
   black pepper

1. Preheat the oven to 200C/400F/gas 6 and line a baking tray with parchment paper.

2. Place all of the chopped vegetables on the baking tray, then drizzle over the oil and sprinkle generously with salt and pepper. Toss well to combine.

3. Roast for 35 to 45 minutes, until the squash is tender, then serve hot!

# SESAME-SPRINKLED GARLIC & SPRING ONION BROCCOLI

Not your usual steamed or boiled broccoli, this dish gets a kick of garlic, spring onion and toasted sesame oil along with lots of crunch from a handful of sesame seeds. Blanching the broccoli quickly and then popping it into an ice bath preserves its nutrients and prevents it from turning to mush, while sautéing it quickly in the sesame, garlic and spring onion mixture crisps it up just a little around the edges and infuses it with gorgeous flavours.

*serves 4 as a side*

**10 MINUTES PREPARATION TIME**
**10 MINUTES COOKING TIME**

300g tenderstem or purple sprouting broccoli
1 tablespoon coconut oil
2 teaspoons toasted sesame oil
2 cloves of garlic, thinly sliced
1 spring onion, thinly sliced
1 tablespoon coconut aminos (see page 23) or gluten-free tamari
a small handful of sesame seeds

1. Bring a saucepan of hot water to the boil, then add the broccoli and blanch for 3 to 4 minutes, until tender. Meanwhile, prepare a big bowl of cold water and ice, and transfer the broccoli to the ice bath as soon as it's done cooking.

2. Heat the coconut oil and sesame oil in a frying pan over a medium heat, then add the garlic and spring onion and sauté for a minute or two, until fragrant. Add the coconut aminos, broccoli and sesame seeds and toss for 3 to 4 minutes, until the broccoli is warmed through and tender. Serve immediately.

# EVERYDAY EATS

With everything from 10-minute meals to homemade curries, there is something for everyone here, whether you're running around all day and in need of a quick, healthy dinner or want to spend a little longer in the kitchen to whip up a feast. There are really simple yet flavour-packed ideas if you're completely new to cooking, but I've also included some slightly more challenging ones to keep things interesting yet still approachable. Get into the kitchen and start cooking yourself some wholesome, nutritious and delicious eats!

# APRICOT & MINT CHICKEN ROMAINE BOATS

Inspired by the British classic Coronation chicken with a fresh Moroccan twist from the mint, these romaine boats are full of great flavour. With a silky coconut milk dressing, chunks of sweet, juicy apricot and crisp lettuce, they're best served chilled, so give them an hour or two in the fridge before serving if you can! If apricots aren't in season, use apples or grapes instead.

*serves 4*

**10 MINUTES PREPARATION TIME**

60ml (¼ cup) full-fat tinned
  coconut milk
1 tablespoon lemon juice
¼ teaspoon cayenne pepper
a pinch of fine sea salt and freshly
ground black pepper
1 teaspoon coconut oil
2 skinless, boneless chicken
  breasts, cubed
a handful of flaked almonds
2 fresh apricots, pitted and
  roughly chopped
2 spring onions, chopped
a handful of mint, chopped
a small romaine lettuce (or
  little gem)

1. Stir together the coconut milk, lemon juice, cayenne and a pinch each of sea salt and black pepper in a small bowl. Pop this dressing into the fridge to thicken up while you prepare the rest of the dish.

2. Heat the coconut oil in a frying pan over a medium heat, then sauté the cubed chicken breast for 5 to 6 minutes, until fully cooked and golden. Transfer the chicken to a bowl, then add the flaked almonds to the hot pan, toast them for a minute or so, until lightly golden, then set aside.

3. Add the chopped apricots, spring onions and mint to the bowl of cooked chicken and toss to combine. Pour the chilled dressing over the chicken and stir well until everything is evenly coated. Pop the mixture into the fridge for an hour or two if you have time.

4. Right before serving, spoon the chicken mixture into the lettuce leaves and sprinkle with the toasted flaked almonds. Enjoy!

# ORANGE-GINGER BEEF, BROCCOLI & BOK CHOY STIR-FRY

I love a good stir-fry – they're full of flavour, quick to prepare and are one of the best ways to cook veg, as they retain all their nutrients and just a little crunch. The combination of orange, ginger, garlic, sesame, honey and coconut aminos infuses the beef strips with a kick of flavour (although if you like things very spicy, feel free to add a chopped red chilli to the marinade as well!), while lots of colourful broccoli, red pepper, carrot and bok choy pack the meal with nutrients.

*serves 4*

**15 MINUTES PREPARATION TIME**
**15 MINUTES COOKING TIME**

zest and juice of 1
    unwaxed orange
2 tablespoons coconut aminos
    (see page 23) or gluten-free
    tamari
a 5cm piece of ginger, peeled
    and chopped
2 cloves of garlic, finely chopped
1 teaspoon honey
1 teaspoon sesame oil
400g sirloin, rump or fillet
    steak, sliced
2 tablespoons coconut oil
200g broccoli florets or purple
    sprouting broccoli
1 red pepper, thinly sliced
2 medium carrots, peeled and
    julienned (see page 29)
1 baby bok choy, cored and
    thinly sliced
a pinch of fine sea salt and
    freshly ground black pepper

**TO GARNISH:**
sesame seeds and chopped
    spring onions

1. Put the orange zest, orange juice, coconut aminos, chopped ginger and garlic, honey and sesame oil into a bowl or a resealable bag. Add the sliced steak and mix well to evenly disperse the flavours. Cover the bowl or seal the bag and pop into the fridge for at least an hour to marinate.

2. Heat 1 tablespoon of coconut oil in a big frying pan (or a wok if you've got one) over a high heat, then add the broccoli, red pepper and carrots. Sauté, tossing the veg often, for a few minutes, until they start to soften, then add the bok choy and a pinch of sea salt and black pepper and sauté for another minute or so, until the bok choy is tender and the other veg are cooked yet still have a bit of crunch. Transfer the veg to a bowl and set aside. While the pan is hot, add a handful of sesame seeds and toast them for about a minute, until golden and fragrant. Set these aside in a small bowl to use as garnish.

3. Heat another tablespoon of coconut oil in the same pan, then add the marinated contents of the bag or bowl and sauté for a few minutes, until browned and cooked. Take the veg you set aside earlier and add them back to the pan, tossing a few times to mix them with the seasoned beef, then sprinkle generously with the toasted sesame seeds and a chopped spring onion to garnish. Serve immediately.

# GARLIC & CHILLI CHICKEN SKEWERS

Packed with fresh garlic and chilli, these skewers only require a few minutes of hands-on time for a great result. I serve them with a side of refreshing tomato, mint & parsley chopped salad (see page 98) or cucumber ribbon, radish, spring onion & sugar snap salad (see page 95). I've used a very simple oil, chilli and garlic marinade to infuse the chicken with fantastic flavour and gives it a gorgeous colour as well!

*serves 4*

**10 MINUTES PREPARATION TIME**
**+ 1 HOUR MARINATING TIME**
**2 MINUTES COOKING TIME**

8 wooden skewers
4 skinless, boneless chicken breasts
2 tablespoons extra virgin olive oil
1 red chilli, deseeded
3 cloves of garlic
a pinch of fine sea salt and freshly
  ground black pepper

1.  Soak the wooden skewers in cold water for about an hour.

2.  Meanwhile, cut the chicken breasts into 2½cm chunks and pop them into a bowl or a resealable bag. Put the olive oil, chilli, garlic, sea salt and black pepper into a food processor and whizz for about a minute, until fully combined.

3.  Pour this marinade mixture over the chicken and stir well so that the chicken is evenly coated, then cover the bowl or close the bag and set in the fridge for 1 hour to allow the flavours to meld.

4.  Once the marinating time is over, remove the chicken from the container and thread the chunks on to the skewers.

5.  To cook the chicken, either pop the skewers on a hot grill for a few minutes, turning often, until fully cooked, or lay them on a lined baking sheet and bake at 180°C/350°F/gas 4 for 20 minutes. Serve hot, with a crisp, refreshing salad!

# SWEET POTATO VEGETABLE PAD THAI WITH LIME, TAHINI & GINGER DRESSING

Packed with all sorts of colourful veg, fresh flavours and a bright, zingy dressing, this healthy remake of a classic Thai favourite is both delicious and stunning, thanks to all the gorgeous colours! If you'd like to add a bit more protein, toss through some leftover roasted chicken when you add the dressing and heat until warmed through.

*serves* 4

**15 MINUTES PREPARATION TIME**
**15 MINUTES COOKING TIME**

1 tablespoon coconut oil
1 clove of garlic, finely chopped
2 shallots, chopped
1 medium sweet potato, peeled and spiralized (or sliced as described on page 86)
¼ of a red cabbage, thinly sliced
2 courgettes, peeled and spiralized (or sliced as described on page 86)
1 carrot, peeled into thin ribbons
a big handful of mangetout
2 spring onions, thinly sliced
a big handful of fresh coriander

**FOR THE LIME, TAHINI & GINGER DRESSING:**
2 teaspoons toasted sesame oil
the juice of 1 lime
a thumb-size piece of fresh ginger, grated
2 tablespoons coconut sugar or unrefined brown sugar
3 tablespoons tahini
3 tablespoons almond butter (see page 40)
3 tablespoons coconut aminos (see page 23) or gluten-free tamari
a pinch each of fine sea salt and freshly ground black pepper
2 tablespoons sesame seeds

1. Start off by making the dressing: stir everything together in a small bowl until well combined, then pop it into the fridge to allow the flavours to meld.

2. Heat the coconut oil in a big frying pan over medium heat, then add the garlic and shallots and sauté for a few minutes, until starting to soften. Add the sweet potato noodles and red cabbage and sauté them for a further few minutes, until the sweet potato noodles have softened but still have a little crunch. Toss in the courgette noodles, carrot ribbons, the dressing, mangetout and spring onion, then toss thoroughly to combine everything and sauté for 2 to 3 minutes to heat up. Serve with plenty of chopped coriander, lime wedges and a sprinkling of sesame seeds.

# SALMON CAKES WITH SPICED CAULIFLOWER RICE

Salmon cakes are fancy without the fuss and they save on the washing up too. The cauliflower rice I serve them with is full of beneficial vitamins – I like to sauté mine to get that lovely nutty taste and golden brown specks throughout. I find that steaming cauliflower rice results in a mushy, bland mess, so if you've tried it steamed and weren't a fan, give this method a go.

*serves 4*

**15 MINUTES PREPARATION TIME**
**10 MINUTES COOKING TIME**

**FOR THE SALMON CAKES:**
4 skinless, boneless salmon fillets
    (about 500g), preferably
    wild caught
2 shallots, roughly chopped
1 spring onion, finely chopped
1 tablespoon Dijon mustard
1 tablespoon extra virgin olive oil
1 stalk of celery, roughly chopped
½ a red pepper, roughly chopped
a pinch of fine sea salt
a handful of fresh parsley

**FOR THE SPICED CAULIFLOWER RICE:**
1 large cauliflower, leaves and stems
    removed and cut into florets
1 tablespoon coconut oil
1 tablespoon curry powder
a big pinch of fine sea salt (this is
    what really brings out the spices,
    so don't skimp!)

1. To make the salmon cakes, put all the ingredients into a food processor and whizz for about a minute, until combined into a sticky mixture with the ingredients evenly dispersed. Form into 8 patties, using your hands, and press them flat until they're about 1 cm thick. Set aside in the fridge while you prepare the cauliflower rice.

2. Pop the cauliflower into a food processor and blitz until it's evenly and finely chopped into rice-size pieces. Alternatively, grate the cauliflower using a box grater.

3. Heat the coconut oil in a frying pan over medium-high heat, then add the curry powder and fry gently for about 30 seconds, stirring often, until fragrant. Add the riced cauliflower and sea salt, spreading out a thin, even layer – this way, it'll brown evenly. Increase the heat to high and sauté for about 5 minutes, until it browns at the edges and is light and fluffy. While you sauté the cauliflower rice, heat a splash of coconut oil in another frying pan over a medium heat, then add the patties and cook for a few minutes on each side, until golden brown and cooked throughout.

4. Serve 2 salmon patties per person with a big scoop of cauliflower rice and a handful of rocket lightly dressed with lemon juice and olive oil for a pop of colour. Garnish with a sprinkling of chopped parsley. Enjoy!

# RED PEPPER CHICKEN FAJITAS WITH BALSAMIC TOMATO SALSA

This is a true family favourite – we've been eating it for years and years and we still can't get enough. It's delicious served in either homemade tortillas (see page 254) or lettuce wraps, but the juicy balsamic tomato salsa and the creamy guacamole are a must!

*serves 4*

**20 MINUTES PREPARATION TIME**
**15 MINUTES COOKING TIME**

**FOR THE RED PEPPER CHICKEN MIXTURE:**
1 tablespoon extra virgin olive oil
4 shallots, finely chopped
2 cloves of garlic
2 red peppers, halved, deseeded and thinly sliced
4 skinless, boneless chicken breasts, finely sliced
a big pinch of fine sea salt and freshly ground black pepper

**FOR THE BALSAMIC TOMATO SALSA:**
6 medium tomatoes
½ a cucumber
1 tablespoon extra virgin olive oil
¾ tablespoon balsamic vinegar
a pinch of fine sea salt

**TO SERVE:**
a batch of guacamole (see page 250)
a double batch of homemade tortilla wraps (see page 254), or 2 little gem lettuces

1. Make the balsamic salsa by first cutting the tomatoes in half, scooping out the seeds and discarding them. Pop the deseeded tomatoes, cucumber, olive oil, balsamic and sea salt into a food processor and pulse a few times, until combined but still a little chunky – you don't want it to turn into mush!

2. Transfer the salsa to a bowl, then make the guacamole while the food processor is out – you don't have to wash it up after making the salsa, as any salsa left in there adds a nice flavour to the guacamole. Set the bowls of guacamole and balsamic salsa in the fridge until you're ready to serve. If you're opting for the tortillas, make those now as well, so that all you have to do is heat them up again right before serving. If you're using lettuce wraps have them all washed and ready to go.

3. To make the chicken mixture, heat the olive oil in a frying pan over a medium heat, then add the shallots and garlic and sauté for 2 to 3 minutes, until starting to soften. Add your sliced peppers, the sliced chicken breast and a pinch of sea salt and black pepper, then sauté for another 5 to 10 minutes, until the chicken is golden and fully cooked.

4. I like to serve all the different parts of this dish in bowls and pop them in the middle of the table, so that everyone can build their own fajitas by grabbing a lettuce leaf or a homemade tortilla and piling it high with a scoop of the roasted red pepper chicken, a dollop of guacamole and a spoonful of balsamic salsa.

# ALMOND & LEMON-CRUSTED WILD SALMON WITH ROASTED VINE TOMATOES & LEMONY GREENS

I absolutely love wild salmon – it contains lots of omega-3 fatty acids which are brilliant for radiant skin, and vitamin B12. The tender, flaky salmon combined with the crunchy, bright almond and lemon crust along with plenty of vibrant veg makes this one of my favourite meals – impressive yet simple, and I love that it's ready in just 15 minutes. The recipe will work just as well with farmed salmon if that's all you can source, and try using pistachios instead of the almonds for a tasty variation!

*serves 4*

**5 MINUTES PREPARATION TIME**
**10 MINUTES COOKING TIME**

**FOR THE SALMON:**
2 teaspoons Dijon mustard
the juice of ½ a lemon
zest of 1 lemon
a big handful of flaked
   almonds, chopped
1 tablespoon extra virgin olive oil
a few sprigs of dill, finely chopped
fine sea salt and freshly ground
   black pepper
4 wild-caught salmon fillets

**FOR THE ROASTED TOMATOES:**
4 stalks (about 300g) of
   cherry tomatoes
a drizzle of extra virgin olive oil
fine sea salt and freshly ground
   black pepper

**FOR THE LEMONY GREENS:**
a very big handful each of
   watercress, rocket and spinach
the juice of ½ a lemon
2 tablespoons extra virgin olive oil

1. Preheat oven to 200°C/400°F/gas 6 and line a baking sheet with parchment paper.

2. Combine the mustard, lemon juice and zest, chopped almonds, extra virgin olive oil, dill and a pinch of sea salt and black pepper in a small bowl. Lay the salmon fillets on the lined baking sheet and divide the lemon almond mixture between them, spreading it over with a spoon.

3. Pop the cherry tomatoes on the stalk on the baking sheet as well, drizzle with a little olive oil and sprinkle with a bit of sea salt and black pepper, then put the baking sheet in the oven for 10 to 12 minutes, depending on the thickness of your salmon, until the fish is fully cooked and the tomatoes are starting to char slightly.

4. Meanwhile, mix together all the ingredients for the lemony greens in a big bowl.

5. Serve each salmon fillet with a stalk of roasted tomatoes and a handful of greens.

# MEXICAN BURGERS WITH ALL THE TOPPINGS & RAW BEETROOT-CARROT SLAW

This dish just screams summer to me — juicy burgers with a refreshing salsa relish made with lots of seasonal veg, along with a colourful raw beetroot and carrot slaw. I love serving these in lettuce cups for extra crunch.

*serves 4*

**15 MINUTES PREPARATION TIME**
**15 MINUTES COOKING TIME**

**FOR THE MEXICAN BURGERS:**
500g minced beef
1 ½ teaspoons chili powder
1 teaspoon ground cumin
½ teaspoon paprika
1 teaspoon arrowroot starch
a big pinch of fine sea salt and
  freshly ground black pepper
1 tablespoon coconut oil, for frying

**FOR THE SALSA RELISH:**
2 large tomatoes, deseeded
  and diced
1 cucumber, diced
1 spring onion, thinly sliced
1 red pepper, deseeded and diced
a splash of olive oil
the juice of ½ a lime

**FOR THE BEETROOT-CARROT SLAW:**
1 large beetroot, peeled
2 large carrots, peeled
1 tablespoon extra virgin olive oil
1 teaspoon apple cider vinegar
¼ teaspoon Dijon mustard

**TO SERVE:**
a batch of guacamole (see page 250)

**OPTIONAL:**
crispy fried shallots (see page 84)
fresh lettuce leaves

1. Mix together all the burger ingredients except for the coconut oil in a big bowl and form the mixture into 8 patties. Don't worry about making them perfectly round — part of the appeal of homemade burgers is their rustic look! Pop them into the fridge while you prepare the rest of the meal.

2. Make the salsa relish by mixing together the ingredients in a big bowl, then set aside to allow the flavours to meld. Prepare the guacamole and crispy fried shallots (if using).

3. To make the beetroot-carrot slaw, put the raw beetroot and carrots through a food processor fitted with a grating blade (you can grate them by hand as well, but your hands will be stained for days — you've been warned!), then transfer the shredded veg to a bowl, add the remaining ingredients and toss together to combine.

4. To cook the burgers, heat the coconut oil in a frying pan over a medium-high heat, then add the burgers and cook for 3 to 4 minutes on each side, until browned and cooked through but still juicy. You can also grill them if you want. Top the burgers with plenty of guacamole and salsa relish and serve on lettuce leaves, with a big spoonful of beetroot-carrot slaw on the side and some crispy fried shallots, if you like.

# ROASTED POLLACK WITH RED PEPPER, TOMATOES & CHILLI WITH PESTO-DRIZZLED HASSELBACK SWEET POTATOES

This dish can be thrown together in just over an hour and doesn't require much effort or any fancy ingredients. Hasselback sweet potatoes are one of my favourite ways to serve them – they're very thinly sliced, so they fan out and become gloriously crispy at the edges but tender inside. While they look quite tricky to make, they're actually very easy. Pollack is a delicious, sustainable white-fleshed fish that can be found at most fishmongers and supermarkets. Roasting it in a fragrant mixture packed with garlic, chilli and red onion infuses it with delicious Mediterranean-inspired flavours and only requires 10 minutes of hands-on work!

*serves 4*

**10 MINUTES PREPARATION TIME**
**75 MINUTES COOKING TIME**

**FOR THE HASSELBACK SWEET POTATOES:**
4 medium sweet potatoes, peeled
2 tablespoons extra virgin olive oil
½ teaspoon garlic powder
a very big pinch of fine sea salt
a batch of homemade pesto
  (see page 248)

**FOR THE ROASTED POLLACK:**
2 tablespoons extra virgin olive oil
2 cloves of garlic, finely chopped
1 red onion, finely chopped
1 red pepper, deseeded and
  thinly sliced
400g cherry tomatoes, halved
1 tablespoon tomato paste
a small pinch of chilli powder or
  chilli flakes
a pinch of fine sea salt and freshly
  ground black pepper
4 skinless, boneless sustainably sourced
  pollack fillets, about 140g each
a handful of basil leaves, chiffonaded
  (see page 29)

1. Preheat the oven to 200°C/400°F/gas 6. To prepare the sweet potatoes grab two chopsticks or pencils and place them horizontally, about 5cm apart, on a chopping board. Pop a peeled sweet potato in the middle so that the edges are just touching the chopsticks/pencils, then use a sharp knife to slice down vertically into the sweet potato – the chopsticks or pencils will stop you cutting completely through. Keep making cuts as closely together as you can until you end up with a sweet potato 'fan', then repeat for the remaining sweet potatoes. Pop them on to a baking sheet lined with parchment paper, drizzle with the olive oil, sprinkle generously with sea salt and the garlic powder, then place in the oven to roast for about 1 hour and 15 minutes, until completely tender (you can check this by poking a sharp knife into the middle of one slice – it should glide in and out very easily when fully cooked). ➤

**2.** To make the sauce for the roasted pollack, heat the olive oil in an ovenproof casserole or frying pan over a medium heat, then add the garlic, red onion, red pepper, cherry tomatoes, tomato paste, chilli, sea salt and black pepper. Sauté for about 10 minutes, stirring often, until the tomatoes and peppers have softened. Remove from the heat and set aside until the sweet potatoes are almost done cooking – I wait until they've got about 15 minutes left, so that everything will be done at the same time. Meanwhile, make the pesto to drizzle over the sweet potatoes.

**3.** Place your pollack fillets in the pan with the tomato and pepper mixture. Pop the pan into the oven for about 15 minutes, until the pollack is fully cooked but still tender and flaky. Sprinkle over the chiffonaded basil leaves, then generously drizzle the hasselback sweet potatoes with pesto as soon as they're out of the oven.

**4.** Serve the pollack fillets with a big scoop of the tomato and pepper mixture along with a pesto-covered hasselback sweet potato. Enjoy!

# MEATBALLS IN MOROCCAN TOMATO SAUCE WITH COURGETTE NOODLES

I've paired simple, lightly spiced meatballs with a Moroccan-inspired 10-minute tomato sauce to amp up the flavour, and served it over fresh courgette noodles for a nutrient-packed twist on the classic spag bol. Use minced chicken, turkey or pork instead of beef if you fancy, or serve the meatballs on a cocktail stick with the tomato sauce as a dip!

*serves 4*

**15 MINUTES PREPARATION TIME**
**25 MINUTES COOKING TIME**

**FOR THE MEATBALLS:**
500g minced beef (preferably
  organic and grass-fed)
a pinch of fine sea salt and
  freshly ground black pepper
½ teaspoon garlic powder
1 tablespoon extra virgin olive oil
½ tablespoon tomato paste
½ tablespoon arrowroot
1 teaspoon ground coriander
1 teaspoon chilli powder
1 teaspoon ground cumin
a splash of coconut oil, for frying

**FOR THE MOROCCAN
TOMATO SAUCE:**
1 tablespoon coconut oil
1 clove of garlic, chopped
2 shallots, chopped
1 teaspoon harissa paste
2 teaspoons ground cumin
1 teaspoon ground coriander
a pinch of chilli powder
a big pinch of fine sea salt and
  freshly ground black pepper
2 x 400ml tins of chopped tomatoes

**FOR THE COURGETTE NOODLES:**
4 courgettes, peeled and spiralized
  (or sliced as described on page 86)

1. Make the meatballs by combining all the ingredients except the coconut oil in a big bowl using your hands. Shape and roll into golf ball-size meatballs, then repeat until all the mixture is used up.

2. Heat a splash of coconut oil in a frying pan over a medium heat, then add the meatballs and sauté for about 10 minutes, until they're golden brown and cooked through. Remove from the pan and set aside on a plate.

3. Make the tomato sauce by heating the coconut oil in the same frying pan, then adding the garlic, shallots, harissa paste, spices, sea salt and black pepper. Sauté for 2 to 3 minutes, until the shallots are starting to soften, then add the tinned tomatoes. Stir well, then reduce the heat to low and let the sauce simmer for about 10 minutes.

4. Meanwhile, bring a saucepan of hot water to the boil and add the courgette noodles. Cook for 2 to 3 minutes, until just tender, then strain.

5. Add the meatballs to the tomato sauce, stir well and simmer for another minute or so until heated through. Serve over the courgette noodles.

# EGYPTIAN DUKKAH-CRUSTED CHICKEN FILLETS WITH CAULIFLOWER TABBOULEH

Dukkah is an Egyptian spice mix made with just a few ingredients, but it's one of my absolute favourite flavour combinations. You'll only need a few spoonfuls of dukkah for this recipe, so keep the leftovers in a sealed glass jar and use it to sprinkle over eggs or salads to add a delicious crunch and lots of flavour! This tabbouleh is one of my favourite ways to enjoy cauliflower – it's simple but delicious.

*serves 4*

**15 MINUTES PREPARATION TIME**
**30 MINUTES COOKING TIME**

**FOR THE DUKKAH:**
80g (½ cup) raw hazelnuts
65g (½ cup) sesame seeds
20g (¼ cup) coriander seeds
20g (¼ cup) cumin seeds
a big pinch of fine sea salt

**FOR THE CHICKEN FILLETS:**
2 tablespoons coconut oil
4 tablespoons dukkah (recipe above, or use a shop-bought version if short on time)
4 chicken breast fillets (about 150g each)

**FOR THE CAULIFLOWER TABBOULEH:**
1 medium cauliflower, leaves and stems removed and cut into florets
about 100g fresh parsley, chopped
200g cherry tomatoes, halved
1 red pepper, diced
1 cucumber, diced
3 spring onions, thinly sliced
2 tablespoons extra virgin olive oil
the juice of ½ a lemon
a pinch of fine sea salt and freshly ground black pepper

**OPTIONAL:**
seeds of ½ a pomegranate

1. Preheat the oven to 180°C/350°F/gas 4 and line a baking sheet with parchment paper.

2. To make the dukkah, put all the ingredients into a frying pan over a medium heat and toast, stirring often, for 5 to 6 minutes, until fragrant and starting to brown slightly. Blitz in a food processor for about 10 seconds, until finely ground.

3. Rub the chicken all over with the coconut oil, then sprinkle over the dukkah and press until the fillets are completely coated. Roast the chicken on a lined baking sheet for 25 minutes, until the chicken is fully cooked. Leave to cool for a few minutes, then slice ready to serve on top of the tabbouleh.

4. Make the tabbouleh by whizzing the cauliflower florets in a food processor for 20 to 30 seconds, until chopped into rice-sized bits. Transfer these to a big bowl, then rinse out the food processor. Put the parsley, cherry tomatoes, red pepper, cucumber and spring onions into the processor and blitz. Transfer to the bowl of cauliflower. Toss well, then drizzle over the olive oil, lemon juice and a sprinkle of sea salt and black pepper. Toss again, then top with pomegranate seeds to garnish.

5. Serve slices of the chicken alongside a big scoop of the cauliflower tabbouleh and enjoy!

# DILL & CHIVE FISH PATTIES WITH CRISPY SPICED SWEET POTATO FRIES

Simple yet packed full of flavour, these patties are a really nutrient-packed, high-protein meal. I've paired them with baked sweet potato fries for a healthier take on fish and chips! Try to use wild-caught, sustainably sourced fish wherever possible.

*serves 4*

**15 MINUTES PREPARATION TIME**
**30 MINUTES COOKING TIME**

**FOR THE FISH PATTIES:**
200g fresh cod fillets
200g fresh salmon fillets
200g undyed smoked haddock
1 tablespoon of chopped fresh dill
1 tablespoon of chopped fresh chives
a pinch each of fine sea salt and freshly ground black pepper
1 tablespoon arrowroot
a little coconut oil, for frying
½ a lemon cut into wedges and a small handful of chives, chopped, to garnish

**FOR THE SWEET POTATO FRIES:**
2 big sweet potatoes
2 tablespoons coconut oil, melted
1 teaspoon garlic powder
1 teaspoon paprika
½ teaspoon dried oregano
a big pinch of sea salt and freshly ground black pepper

**OPTIONAL (IT'S SPICY!):**
a pinch of cayenne pepper

1. To make the fries, preheat the oven to 200°C/400°F/gas 6 and line a baking sheet with parchment paper. Peel the sweet potatoes and cut into thin fries – the thinner they are, the crispier they will be! Pop the fries into a big bowl and add the coconut oil, then toss well to combine. In a small bowl, mix together the garlic powder, paprika, oregano, sea salt, black pepper and cayenne (if using), then scatter this spice mixture over the sweet potatoes and toss until they are all evenly coated.

2. Transfer the fries to the baking sheet and arrange in a single layer (try to spread them apart so they're not touching – this makes them crispier). Bake for 25 to 30 minutes, until golden.

3. Meanwhile, make the fish patties. Put all the ingredients except the coconut oil into a food processor and whizz for about a minute. Scrape down the sides with a spoon and blitz again, then grab golfball-size balls of the mixture and use your hands to press them into 1cm thick patties – you should be able to make about a dozen.

4. When the sweet potato fries are almost done cooking, start frying the fish patties. Heat a little coconut oil in two frying pans over a medium heat, and cook the patties for 2 to 3 minutes on each side, until golden.

5. Serve the fish patties and sweet potato fries immediately, with some fresh lemon wedges and a garnish of chopped chives if you wish. Leftover fish patties keep well in an airtight container in the fridge for up to 2 days.

# SPICED CHOCOLATE CHILLI WITH CORIANDER-SPIKED AVOCADO

The secret to a great chilli is adding a little bit of chocolate – I know it sounds odd, but it's true! Hearty and filling, this one is full of smoky spices and goes perfectly with coriander-spiked avocado.

*serves 4*

**10 MINUTES PREPARATION TIME**
**45 MINUTES COOKING TIME**

**FOR THE SPICED CHOCOLATE CHILLI:**
1 tablespoon coconut oil
3 shallots, finely chopped
2 cloves of garlic, finely chopped
1 stalk of celery, finely chopped
2 medium carrots, finely chopped
1 red pepper, deseeded and
  finely chopped
1–2 teaspoons chilli powder,
  (depending on how spicy you'd like
  it to be)
1 teaspoon ground cumin
¼ teaspoon each cayenne powder
  and ground cloves
½ teaspoon each ground oregano,
  ground cinnamon, marjoram
  and thyme
a big pinch of fine sea salt and
  freshly ground black pepper
500g high-quality minced beef
1 x 400g tin of chopped tomatoes
1 tablespoon tomato purée
1 teaspoon cacao powder
250ml (1 cup) chicken or vegetable
  stock, or 1 homemade chicken or
  vegetable stock cube (see pages
  76–79) dissolved in 250ml (1 cup)
  boiling water

**FOR THE AVOCADO:**
2 ripe avocados, halved and pitted
the juice of ½ a lime

1. Heat the coconut oil in a casserole pan or large frying pan over medium heat, then add the shallots and garlic and sauté for 2 to 3 minutes, until starting to soften. Stir in the celery, carrots and red pepper, then fry for another 2 to 3 minutes, stirring often. Add the chilli powder, cumin, cayenne, cloves, oregano, cinnamon, marjoram, thyme and a big pinch of sea salt and black pepper, stir to combine, then add the minced beef.

2. Fry for about 5 minutes, breaking the mince up with a spoon or spatula as you cook it, until browned throughout, then add the chopped tomatoes, tomato purée, cacao powder and stock and stir well.

3. Bring to a simmer, then reduce the heat to low, cover the pot with the lid askew and cook for 30 minutes.

4. Serve the chilli hot, with half an avocado squeezed with a little lime juice, sprinkled with sea salt and chopped coriander and with a simple salad on the side.

# HONEY SESAME CHICKEN WITH BABY BOK CHOY

I love a bowl of this sticky honey sesame chicken – it's simple but absolutely packed with flavour. Alongside quickly sautéd baby bok choy with lots of ginger, this is a delicious supper. If you'd like to make it a little more filling, serve with a side of spiced cauliflower rice (see page 124) or sweet potato chips (see page 141).

*serves 4*

**15 MINUTES PREPARATION TIME**
**15 MINUTES COOKING TIME**

**FOR THE HONEY SESAME CHICKEN:**
1 teaspoon coconut oil
4 boneless, skinless chicken
   breasts, sliced
2 tablespoons honey
a pinch of fine sea salt and freshly
   ground black pepper
2 tablespoons coconut aminos (see
   page 23) or gluten-free tamari
125ml (½ cup) water
1 tablespoon arrowroot
a handful of sesame seeds

**FOR THE BABY BOK CHOY:**
1 teaspoon coconut oil
1 clove of garlic, finely chopped
a small piece of fresh ginger, peeled
   and grated
a pinch of fine sea salt and freshly
   ground black pepper
4 baby bok choy, chopped

1. For the chicken, heat the coconut oil in a frying pan over medium heat, then add the sliced chicken and sauté for 5 to 7 minutes, until golden and cooked. Meanwhile, stir the remaining ingredients except for the sesame seeds together in a small bowl. Once the chicken is cooked, add this sauce mixture to the pan and cook for a further 5 minutes, until the sauce is thick and coats the chicken, then sprinkle with the sesame seeds.

2. In the last 5 minutes of cooking the chicken, cook the bok choy by heating the coconut oil in another frying pan over a medium heat, then add the garlic, ginger, sea salt and black pepper and stir for a minute. Add the chopped baby bok choy and cook for another 4 to 6 minutes, until the greens are wilted and the stems have just a bit of crunch left.

3. Serve the honey sesame chicken alongside the baby bok choy.

# SAFFRON KING PRAWNS & GARLIC-CHILLI COURGETTE NOODLES

Fast, delicious and healthy, this is one of my favourite 15-minute meals! With saffron-infused coconut milk and flavour-packed shallots, spring onions and chilli, the prawns are absolutely delicious and even more so when served over the garlic-chilli courgette noodles. Buy peeled and deveined, sustainably sourced king prawns if you can, as it's very fiddly to remove the shells and veins yourself.

*serves 4*

**15 MINUTES PREPARATION TIME**

**FOR THE SAFFRON PRAWNS:**
125ml (½ cup) full-fat tinned
  coconut milk
a pinch of saffron
1 tablespoon coconut oil
2 shallots, finely chopped
3 cloves of garlic, finely chopped
1 red chilli, thinly sliced
½ teaspoon chilli flakes (optional)
3 spring onions, very thinly sliced
350g king prawns, peeled
  and deveined
the juice of ½ a lime
a pinch of fine sea salt and freshly
  ground black pepper

**FOR THE COURGETTE NOODLES:**
1 tablespoon coconut oil
2 cloves of garlic, finely chopped
a pinch of red chilli flakes
3 large courgettes, spiralized (or
  sliced as described on page 86)

**TO GARNISH:**
a thinly sliced chilli, lime wedges and
  some chopped spring onion

1. In a small saucepan, heat the coconut milk and saffron, stirring constantly, until simmering, then remove from the heat and set aside.

2. Heat the coconut oil in a frying pan over medium heat, then add the shallots, garlic, chilli, chilli flakes (if using) and spring onions and sauté for 2 to 3 minutes, until fragrant and starting to soften. Add the king prawns and sauté for a further 2 to 3 minutes, until the prawns are opaque and cooked. Take them off the heat when they're done to prevent overcooking them.

3. Meanwhile, heat another frying pan over a medium heat and heat the coconut oil for the courgette noodles. Add the garlic and red chilli flakes and sauté those for about 2 minutes, then add the courgette noodles, stirring often for another minute to soften them slightly.

4. Going back to the prawns, add the lime juice, a little sea salt and black pepper and the saffron-infused coconut milk, and toss to warm through.

5. Serve the saffron prawns over the courgette noodles and garnish with thinly sliced chilli, lime wedges and some chopped spring onion.

# PEA & PEPPER BEEF CURRY

Serve on its own, with a homemade tortilla wrap (see page 254) or on top of a pile of spiced cauliflower rice. You can also bulk it out a bit more by adding sliced carrots, broccoli or cauliflower along with the peppers.

*serves 4*

**15 MINUTES PREPARATION TIME**
**15 MINUTES COOKING TIME**

4 skirt, rump or sirloin steaks (about 200g each), with any big chunks of fat trimmed off
2 tablespoons Thai red curry paste
1 teaspoon coconut oil
2 shallots, finely chopped
2 cloves of garlic, finely chopped
a thumb-size piece of fresh ginger, grated
2 red peppers, deseeded and thinly sliced
300g (1 cup) frozen peas
1 x 400ml tin of full-fat coconut milk
a pinch of fine sea salt and freshly ground black pepper
1 tsp coconut aminos or gluten-free tamari (see page 23)
a handful of fresh coriander, chopped
a lime, cut into wedges, to serve

1. Pop the sliced steak in to a bowl or ziploc bag, then add the curry paste and massage it into the steak. Cover the bowl or seal the bag and pop in the fridge for at least 15 minutes, or if you're making it ahead of time, up to a few hours.

2. Heat the coconut oil in a frying pan over medium heat, then add the shallots, garlic, ginger, red peppers and peas and saute for 3 to 4 minutes, until they are starting to soften. Add the marinated steak and fry for 2 to 3 minutes, until fragrant, then add the tin of coconut milk along with the seasoning and coconut aminos or gluten-free tamari. Bring everything to a simmer, stirring often, for a few minutes, until the beef is cooked. Taste, then add another spoonful of curry paste and mix it in well if you would like it a little spicier.

3. Stir in the coriander and serve immediately, with a wedge of lime on the side.

# PARTY BITES

Everyone loves finger food, and bringing a big plate of healthier snacks is great for showing your friends that healthy food doesn't have to taste like cardboard. Nobody will miss the crisps when you've got cucumber veg rolls with a spicy avocado dip, and forget about the sugar-laden fizzy drinks . . . pomegranate, lime & raspberry spritzers taste ten times as good.

# FUDGY RASPBERRY CHOCOLATE TARTLETS WITH CACAO & TOASTED PECAN CRUST

Decadent and seriously delicious, these little tartlets have a fudgy, gooey cacao and toasted pecan crust filled with a rich chocolatey filling, topped with a fresh raspberry for a healthier twist on this classic flavour combination. Apart from the toasted pecans, they're also completely raw, which means they're great for beginners as you don't need to worry about burning them! I think these look absolutely adorable as little tartlets, but you can certainly make the recipe as a big tart – just press the base mixture into a 23cm loose-based tart tin instead.

*makes 24*

**15 MINUTES PREPARATION TIME + 3 HOURS CHILLING TIME**

**FOR THE CACAO & TOASTED PECAN BASE:**
120g (1 cup) raw pecans
35g (1/3 cup) cacao powder
180g (1 cup) soft, squishy dates, pitted
2 tablespoons maple syrup

**FOR THE CHOCOLATE & RASPBERRY FILLING:**
100g high-quality dark chocolate or dark chocolate chips (see page 24)
80ml (1/3 cup) full-fat tinned coconut milk
1/2 teaspoon vanilla bean powder
1 tablespoon maple syrup
about 150g fresh raspberries

1. Start by making the base: preheat the oven to 180°C/350F/gas 4, then spread the pecans out on a baking sheet and pop them in for 5 minutes to toast, until fragrant and just starting to turn a little darker in colour. Transfer to a food processor, then add the remaining base ingredients and whizz for a few minutes, until combined. The mixture should stick together when you pinch it between your fingers. Press the mixture into a lined mini muffin tray to form about 24 miniature crusts, then pop into the freezer for 15 minutes to firm up.

2. Meanwhile, make the filling by putting the dark chocolate, coconut milk, vanilla bean powder and maple syrup into a small saucepan over a very low heat. Melt together, stirring often, for a few minutes, until combined into a smooth, silky mixture. It won't look very good at first, but it'll come together once all the chocolate is melted! Divide the filling between the chilled crusts, then top each tartlet with a fresh raspberry. Pop into the fridge for 3 hours, then remove from the mini muffin tray and either serve immediately or place in an airtight container and store in the fridge for up to 3 days. These are definitely best served straight from the fridge!

*tip* You can also store these in an airtight container in the freezer for a quick bite. Let them sit at room temperature for half an hour to soften a bit before you dig in!

# SALTED CARAMEL BROWNIES

Gooey and chocolatey, these brownies are definitely a requirement at times! The unrefined coconut sugar in the brownies themselves adds a toffee-like taste and the salted caramel drizzled on top takes it to another level. Try to use the best-quality dark chocolate you can here (preferably homemade – you can find the recipe on page 24).

*makes 12*

**20 MINUTES PREPARATION TIME**
**25 MINUTES COOKING TIME**

200g high-quality dark chocolate or
   dark chocolate chips (see page 24)
60ml (¼ cup) coconut oil or
   unsalted butter
75g (¾ cup) ground almonds
2 tablespoons arrowroot
1 teaspoon vanilla extract
2 medium eggs
105g (¾ cup) coconut sugar or
   unrefined brown sugar
1 batch of salted caramel sauce
   (see page 260)

1. Preheat the oven to 180°C/350°F/gas 4.

2. In a large bowl set over a pan of simmering water, melt the chocolate and coconut oil together.

3. Remove the bowl from the pan, then add all the remaining ingredients except for the salted caramel sauce and whisk very well until fully combined.

4. Line a 20 × 20cm baking tin with parchment paper and grease it with a little coconut oil. Pour the brownie batter into the lined baking tin, then bake for 25 minutes. Meanwhile, make the salted caramel sauce.

5. Let the brownies cool for 10 minutes before removing them from the tin and cutting them into 12 equal pieces. Either serve them warm with a generous drizzle of salted caramel sauce, or keep them in an airtight container for up to 3 days and serve at room temperature with the sauce.

# CUMIN & COURGETTE CHICKEN POPPERS

With vibrant colours and super-nutritious courgettes, these little poppers are both adorable and delicious. The ground cumin gives them a kick and ups their iron content, while the courgette provides vitamin C. Use higher-welfare, free-range chicken wherever possible, and feel free to use chicken mince instead of making your own to save a bit of time!

*makes 12*

**10 MINUTES PREPARATION TIME**
**10 MINUTES COOKING TIME**

2 skinless, boneless chicken breasts, about 150g each
1 medium courgette, grated using a box grater
2 shallots, chopped
a small handful of fresh coriander, chopped
1 clove of garlic, chopped
1 teaspoon ground cumin
a big pinch of fine sea salt
1 tablespoon coconut oil

1. Put the chicken breasts into a food processor and pulse a few times until they turn into mince, then transfer to a bowl. Add the remaining ingredients except the coconut oil and stir very well to combine.

2. Take out a walnut-size scoop of the mixture and quickly roll between your hands to form a ball, then place on a plate and repeat until all of the mixture is used up.

3. Heat the coconut oil in a frying pan over medium heat, then add the chicken balls and sauté for a few minutes, turning often with a pair of tongs, until they're golden and cooked through. Pop them on to cocktail sticks and serve hot – I love these with my guacamole (see page 250) as a dip!

# RAW POMEGRANATE CACAO RIPPLE

I'm asked all the time about the best thing to make if you're new to cooking, and I think this is the winner! It's completely raw (so you can't burn it!), it's made with only a handful of ingredients and it tastes absolutely divine. There's also no need for any fancy equipment and it's easily customizable, so there are endless combinations – use any nut butter you want and replace the pomegranate with fresh or dried berries if you want.

*serves 12*

**10 MINUTES PREPARATION TIME**
**+ 30 MINUTES FREEZING TIME**

60ml (¼ cup) coconut oil, melted
125g (½ cup) almond butter
60ml (¼ cup) maple syrup
35g (⅓ cup) cacao powder
½ teaspoon vanilla bean powder
a handful of coconut flakes
a handful of pomegranate seeds

1. Stir together the coconut oil, almond butter, maple syrup, cacao powder and vanilla bean powder in a medium bowl. Transfer to a lined container, then sprinkle the coconut flakes and pomegranate seeds on top and press them in slightly so they'll stick to the ripple.

2. Freeze for 30 minutes, until firm. Cut into bits with a sharp knife and enjoy! You can store the ripple in an airtight container in the freezer for up to a week.

# PARSLEY & CHIVE PESTO STUFFED MUSHROOMS

A quick and easy finger food, these stuffed mushrooms are packed with vitamins K and C from the fresh herbs. You can make them ahead of time, too – just whizz up the pesto, pop it into a sealed jar in the fridge for up to 2 days, then stuff and bake the mushrooms just before serving. Try to use the freshest herbs you can here for maximum flavour.

*makes 20*

**10 MINUTES PREPARATION TIME**
**15 MINUTES COOKING TIME**

20 chestnut mushrooms,
  stems removed
a big bunch of fresh parsley,
  leaves only
a small bunch of fresh chives
1 clove of garlic, peeled
zest and juice of ½ a lemon
a small handful of toasted pine nuts
a pinch of fine sea salt
4 tablespoons extra virgin olive oil

1. Preheat the oven to 200°C/400°F/gas 6. Quickly rinse the mushrooms, dry them with a paper towel and place them on a baking sheet lined with parchment paper.

2. To make the pesto, whizz the parsley, chives, garlic, lemon zest, lemon juice, pine nuts and sea salt in a food processor until well combined, then add the olive oil one spoonful at a time, whizzing well after each addition, until you have a thick mixture.

3. Use a small spoon to divide the pesto between the mushrooms, then roast for 15 to 20 minutes, until the mushrooms have softened. When they're just out of the oven, sprinkle with a little flaky sea salt (this really brings out the flavours), then serve immediately.

*tip* Make with my traditional basil and pine nut pesto on page 248 if you have some to use up!

# MAPLE MERINGUES WITH COCONUT, BERRIES & PASSIONFRUIT

Meringues are often absolutely loaded with refined sugar, but this version uses maple syrup instead, which is a whole lot better for you and also gives the meringues an extra toasty, caramel-like flavour along with a gorgeous golden colour. Topped with a good dollop of coconut whipped cream, lots of fresh berries and a spoonful of zingy, tropical passionfruit, they're irresistible!

## makes 24

**10 MINUTES PREPARATION TIME**
**2 HOURS COOKING TIME**

**FOR THE MAPLE MERINGUES:**
2 large egg whites
125ml (½ cup) maple syrup
½ teaspoon cream of tartar

**TO SERVE:**
coconut whipped cream (see
 page 256)
plenty of fresh berries
a few passionfruit, pulp scooped out

1. Preheat the oven to 100°C/200°F/gas ¼ and line a baking sheet with parchment paper. Pour a couple of centimetres of hot water into a medium saucepan, then place this over a medium heat and wait until the water simmers.

2. In a heatproof bowl, combine the egg whites, maple syrup and cream of tartar and whisk well until combined. Set the bowl over the pan of simmering water and whisk constantly for a few minutes, until the mixture is warm to the touch.

3. Remove the bowl from the pan, then use an electric whisk or a food mixer with a whisk attachment to whip the egg white mixture for 6 to 8 minutes, until stiff peaks form – that's the one where you can hold the bowl upside down over your head and it won't budge. Once it's stiff, shiny, thick and white, dollop or pipe the meringue mixture on to the baking sheet and use a spoon to smooth them out a little if you want. Bake for an hour, then turn the oven off and leave them in the oven for a further 30 minutes to let them dry and crisp up.

4. To serve, top each meringue with a small spoonful of coconut whipped cream, pile high with fresh berries and drizzle with a spoonful of passionfruit pulp.

# MINI FLAXSEED & OREGANO PIZZAS

These mini pizzas are really great for parties or for sharing with friends, as you can all add your own toppings. You can make both the tomato sauce and the pizza bases in advance. Store the sauce in an airtight container in the fridge and keep the baked pizza bases in an airtight container in the freezer. When you need them, simply add the tomato sauce and toppings to the frozen bases, then pop them into a hot oven for a few minutes to warm through.

*makes 8*

**25 MINUTES PREPARATION TIME**
**15 MINUTES COOKING TIME**

**FOR THE PIZZA BASES:**
2 tablespoons milled flaxseeds
125ml (½ cup) hot water
150g (1 cup) arrowroot
30g (¼ cup) coconut flour
½ teaspoon fine sea salt
1 teaspoon dried oregano
125ml (½ cup) extra virgin olive oil

**FOR THE TOMATO SAUCE:**
125ml (½ cup) tomato paste
60ml (¼ cup) extra virgin olive oil
1 teaspoon garlic powder
1 teaspoon dried oregano
1 teaspoon dried basil
½ teaspoon dried rosemary
½ teaspoon fine sea salt
375ml (1½ cups) water

**OPTIONAL TOPPINGS:**
sliced black olives, pesto, rocket
    leaves, roasted vegetables, cherry
    tomatoes, sautéd mushrooms

1. Preheat the oven to 180°C/350°F/gas 4.

2. To make the pizza bases, grab a large bowl, add the flaxseeds and the hot water, and stir together. Wait a few minutes, until the mixture thickens slightly, then add the remaining pizza base ingredients and knead for a minute or two to form a smooth dough. Wrap the dough in clingfilm and set aside while you prepare the tomato sauce.

3. To make the sauce, combine all the ingredients in a small saucepan and simmer, covered, for 20 minutes. Set aside.

4. Roll the pizza dough between two pieces of parchment paper until it's about ½cm thick. Use a 5cm cookie cutter to cut out 8 mini pizzas, then transfer these to a lined baking tray. Bake for 11 minutes for a chewier crust and 15 minutes for a crispy crust. While the crusts bake, prepare your toppings.

5. As soon as the pizza crusts come out of the oven (they're best hot!), spread them with a thin layer of tomato sauce and add your chosen toppings. Enjoy!

# COOKIE DOUGH STUFFED
# SANDWICH COOKIES

With a chocolate-studded cookie dough filling sandwiched between two rich and fudgy
cookies, these are a huge favourite with my friends, and it's easy to see why! You can
make them in advance if you wish – make the cookies and the filling separately,
then assemble right before serving.

*makes* 16

**10 MINUTES PREPARATION TIME**
**20 MINUTES CHILLING TIME**
**20 MINUTES COOKING TIME**

**FOR THE COOKIES:**
80ml (¹/₃ cup) coconut oil
60ml (¼ cup) almond milk
1 teaspoon ground vanilla
  bean powder
½ teaspoon baking powder
210g (1½ cups) coconut sugar or
  unrefined brown sugar
75g (¾ cup) cacao powder
75g (¾ cup) ground almonds
110g (¾ cup) arrowroot

**FOR THE COOKIE DOUGH FILLING:**
100g (1 cup) ground almonds
2 tablespoons maple syrup
2 tablespoons coconut oil
1 teaspoon vanilla bean powder
50g high-quality chopped dark
  chocolate or dark chocolate chips
  (see page 24)

1. Preheat the oven to 180°C/350°F/gas 4 and line a
baking sheet with parchment paper.

2. Mix together all the cookie ingredients to form a dough,
then pop it into the fridge for about 20 minutes to firm
up a bit. Working quickly, roll the dough out between two
pieces of parchment paper or clingfilm until it's ½cm thick,
then use a small round cookie cutter to cut out cookie
shapes. Transfer them to the baking sheet and bake for
10 to 12 minutes.

3. While they bake, make the cookie dough filling by
mixing together all the ingredients until well combined.

4. Let the cookies cool completely, then take a small
spoonful of the cookie dough filling and sandwich it
between two of the chocolate cookies. Repeat until all
of the cookies and filling have been used up, then serve
immediately and enjoy!

# ALMOND BUTTER CACAO COOKIES

These five-ingredient cookies truly couldn't be any simpler to make – stir together a few ingredients, throw them into the oven and there you go! I consider them pretty much my perfect cookie, thanks to their chewy edges and soft, fudgy middle. When you're making these, ensure that your almond butter has been stirred really well so that it's very creamy and thick – the runnier your almond butter, the more your cookies will fall apart. These cookies freeze very well in an airtight container if you want to make them ahead of time, but they're so easy to put together you might as well make a batch just before serving and enjoy them when they're fresh out of the oven.

*makes* 16

**15 MINUTES PREPARATION TIME**
**10 MINUTES COOKING TIME**

250g (1 cup) roasted almond butter
140g (1 cup) coconut sugar or
  unrefined brown sugar
1 large egg, beaten
35g (⅓ cup) cacao powder
a pinch of bicarbonate of soda

1. Preheat the oven to 180°C/350°F/gas 4 and line a baking sheet with parchment paper.

2. Put all the ingredients into a big bowl and mix very well with your hands to form a dough. Use a spoon or a small ice-cream scoop to dollop the batter on to the lined baking sheet – you should be able to make about 16 cookies. Use the back of a spoon or your fingers to flatten each mound of cookie dough just a little, to ensure that they bake evenly.

3. Bake for 8 to 9 minutes, then remove from the oven and leave to cool for at least 10 minutes (I know it's difficult but it's important!) before you dig in. Best served warm.

*Tip*

Break these cookies up into bits and fold through some coconut milk ice cream (see page 216) to turn into a decadent dessert!

# POMEGRANATE, LIME & RASPBERRY SPRITZERS

A healthier take on a fizzy drink, these refreshing, fruity spritzers are a great way to keep a crowd hydrated. If you're making a big batch, shop-bought pomegranate seeds are a lot less messy, or you can opt for pomegranate juice – make sure it doesn't contain any ingredients other than pomegranate, though, as some brands contain sugars, preservatives and other additives. The blended mixture of pomegranate, raspberries, lime and maple syrup can be made up to 2 hours in advance and kept covered in the fridge until serving, at which point you can add the sparkling water.

*serves 2*

**10 MINUTES PREPARATION TIME**

1 pomegranate (or 1 cup pomegranate seeds or ½ cup pomegranate juice, see above)
a big handful of fresh raspberries
1 tablespoon maple syrup
sparkling water, as needed
a squeeze of lime juice

1. Open the pomegranate and remove the seeds, then pop the seeds, raspberries and maple syrup into a blender and whizz for about 20 seconds, to liquify. Strain the liquid to remove the bits, then divide between 2 tall glasses.

2. Top up the glasses with sparkling water, give them a good stir, taste, adjust the lime juice and maple syrup if necessary, and enjoy immediately! Garnish with a raspberry or two, some pomegranate seeds and a handful of ice if you wish.

*tip*

For a more rustic look (or if you can't be bothered to bring out the blender), just muddle together the pomegranate seeds, raspberries, lime juice and maple syrup in the bottom of the glasses with the end of a rolling pin until mushed together, then top up with sparkling water.

# CUCUMBER VEG ROLLS WITH AVOCADO HERB DIP

A lot more exciting than a plate of crudités, these adorable cucumber veg rolls are ridiculously simple but packed with vibrant, colourful vegetables which are high in vitamins A and C. I love them with this creamy avocado dip, which contains plenty of healthy fats and lots of flavour from all the fresh herbs.

*makes 16*

**15 MINUTES PREPARATION TIME**

**FOR THE ROLLS:**
1 cucumber, ends trimmed off, cut into 5cm long sections
1 red pepper, thinly sliced into 5cm long strips
1 yellow pepper, thinly sliced into 5cm long strips
2 spring onions, sliced into 5cm long strips
1 carrot, peeled and cut into 5cm long sticks

**FOR THE AVOCADO HERB DIP:**
1 avocado, halved, pitted and flesh scooped out
2 spring onions
juice of ½ a lemon
a pinch of sea salt and freshly ground black pepper
a big handful each of chopped fresh chives, parsley and basil
60ml (¼ cup) water

1. Take one of your pieces of cucumber and use an apple corer or a small knife to remove as much of the core as possible. Repeat with the rest of the cucumber, then stand the cored sections vertically.

2. Take your sliced veggies and stuff the cored cucumber sections with them, packing the veggies as tightly together as possible (if you don't, the rolls will fall apart). Once all the cucumber sections are stuffed, lay them down on their sides and slice each 5cm section into four 1cm 'rolls'. Very carefully transfer the rolls to a plate.

3. Make the avocado dip by whizzing all the ingredients together in a food processor or blender until completely smooth, then transfer to a bowl.

4. Serve the rolls with the bowl of dip on the side and enjoy!

# SPINACH & PESTO DEVILLED EGGS

Eggs are incredibly nutritious — jam-packed with protein, as well as being a good source of iron and vitamin A, they're one of the most nourishing foods you can get. With extra greens from the baby spinach and fresh pesto, they're livened up and make a beautiful and delicious snack!

*makes 6*

**15 MINUTES PREPARATION TIME**
**15 MINUTES COOKING TIME**

6 large eggs
a pinch of sea salt
125ml (½ cup) pesto (see page 248)
a handful of baby spinach
2–3 tablespoons almond milk

1. Pop the eggs into a large saucepan, cover with cold water, add a big pinch of sea salt and bring the water to a boil over a high heat. When it boils, turn the heat off, cover the pan with a lid and let the eggs sit for 12 minutes.

2. Rinse the eggs under very cold water, until cooled, then peel. Cut them in half, scoop out the yolks and place them in a food processor or blender. Add the pesto, baby spinach and a bit of the almond milk to the yolks, then whizz. Add more almond milk if needed, to create a completely smooth and creamy mixture. Taste and add a pinch of sea salt if necessary, then either spoon or pipe the mixture back into the egg whites and serve.

# SNACKS

I don't know about you, but I find it hard to last between meals without a pick-me-up, so instead of grazing on everything in sight I like to make myself a quick, easy and satisfying snack. Stocking your cupboards with jars of spicy roasted pumpkin seeds and having a stash of options in the freezer for those days when life gets in the way and I need to eat something now is also one of the ways I deal with snack emergencies ... besides, a box full of chocolate hazelnut fudge at the back of the freezer is never a bad idea!

# HAZELNUT CACAO ENERGY BARS

A great on-the-go snack, these raw bars are a fantastic treat, and they'll only take you a few minutes to whip up. They're full of phosphorus-rich cashews and three types of highly nutritious coconut, so they'll satisfy your chocolate cravings in no time but won't send your blood sugar skyrocketing!  The hazelnut butter inside and decadent layer of dark chocolate on top pack these bars with flavour and make them absolutely irresistible!

*makes 12*

**15 MINUTES PREPARATION TIME**

225g (1½ cups) raw cashews
10 soft and squishy dates, pitted
125g (½ cup) hazelnut butter
  (see page 40)
125ml (½ cup) coconut oil
2 tablespoons maple syrup
60g (½ cup) coconut flour
40g (½ cup) shredded coconut
1 teaspoon vanilla bean powder
100g high-quality dark chocolate or
  dark chocolate chips (see page 24)

**OPTIONAL:**
a handful of flaked almonds

1. Put the raw cashews and dates into a food processor and whizz for 2 to 3 minutes, until very fine.  Add the 2 remaining ingredients except the dark chocolate and flaked almonds, then process for another 2 minutes or so, until the mixture comes together to form a ball and everything is very well combined.

2. Line a rectangular container with parchment paper, then add the bar mixture and press it down evenly.

3. Place the dark chocolate in a bowl and set over a saucepan of simmering water, making sure that the bottom does not touch the water. Stir occasionally until the chocolate is fully melted, then remove the bowl from the pan and pour the melted dark chocolate over the bar mixture. Sprinkle with flaked almonds if you wish, then place the container in the fridge for 3 hours, until set. Slice into 12 small bars, and store them in an airtight container in the fridge for up to a week or in the freezer for up to a month.

# CHERRY ALMOND SQUARES

Studded with juicy fresh cherries, these almond squares are best in the summer months, when cherries are at their peak and in season. If you can't find cherries, fresh berries work just as well!

*makes 16*

**15 MINUTES PREPARATION TIME**
**40 MINUTES COOKING TIME**

200g (2 cups) ground almonds
1 teaspoon baking powder
2 eggs, beaten well
125ml (½ cup) coconut oil
125ml (½ cup) maple syrup
2 teaspoons vanilla extract

**OPTIONAL:**
a few drops of pure almond extract
200g fresh cherries, halved and pitted

1. Preheat the oven to 180°C/350°F/gas 4. Line a 20 x 20cm baking tin with parchment paper, then grease lightly with a little coconut oil.

2. In a large bowl, mix together the ground almonds, baking powder, eggs, coconut oil, maple syrup, vanilla extract and almond extract (if using) to form a batter. Carefully fold in the halved cherries, then transfer the batter to the lined baking tin and smooth it out with the back of a spoon. Bake for 35 to 40 minutes, until golden, then leave to cool for at least half an hour before slicing into 16 squares and enjoying.

3. Leftovers keep well in an airtight container at room temperature for up to 2 days.

# TOASTED MAPLE CINNAMON COCONUT CHIPS

These are so simple but so addictive. Crispy, with a hint of maple, vanilla and cinnamon, they're the perfect snack. Try to find sulphite-free unsweetened coconut flakes – most health food shops and larger supermarkets will stock these. They also make a brilliant crunchy topping for coconut milk ice cream (see page 216)!

*makes 100g*

**5 MINUTES PREPARATION TIME**
**10 MINUTES COOKING TIME**

100g (2 cups) unsweetened
  coconut flakes
2 tablespoons maple syrup
1 teaspoon vanilla bean powder
1 teaspoon ground cinnamon

1. Preheat the oven to 160°C/325°F/gas 3 and line a baking sheet with parchment paper.

2. Mix all the ingredients together in a big bowl and stir until the coconut flakes are evenly coated.

3. Spread the coated coconut flakes on the lined baking sheet and pop into the oven for 10 minutes, stirring halfway through, until the chips are golden brown and toasty. Allow to cool completely, then transfer to a sealed glass jar and keep in the cupboard for up to 2 weeks (although I doubt they'll last that long!).

# WATERMELON, LIME & MINT GRANITA

Granita, a frozen dessert made of flaky ice crystals, is a brilliant way to enjoy a naturally sweet treat on a hot day. I love it – it's very easy to prepare because there is no need for fancy equipment, and, rather than the sugar syrups often used in other recipes, I've used vitamin-packed, thirst-quenching watermelon along with tropical lime and mint for a really delicious and healthy way to enjoy an incredibly refreshing icy treat. Try using fresh berries instead – just be sure to strain the blended mixture to remove any seeds.

*serves 6*

**10 MINUTES PREPARATION TIME
+ 3 HOURS FREEZING TIME**

1 large watermelon (seedless if you
    can find it!)
zest and juice of 1 unwaxed lime
a handful of fresh mint leaves

1. Remove the rind from the watermelon using a sharp knife, then chop the flesh into rough chunks.

2. Add the watermelon to a blender along with the lime zest and juice and the mint leaves, then blend for a minute or two until completely smooth and combined. If your blender doesn't fit all the watermelon, do it in two batches.

3. Pour the mixture into a large shallow container, then cover and freeze for an hour. Use a fork to scrape away the ice crystals at the edges to form little granita flakes, repeat the freezing and scraping process a few times until the whole mixture is made up of small flaky ice crystals and is fully frozen, then serve.

# DATE, CARAMEL & DARK CHOCOLATE SHORTBREAD BARS

I don't think flavour combinations get any better than vanilla bean, caramel and dark chocolate – it's unbeatable! In these bars, you have a tender shortbread base slathered with gooey date caramel and topped with a layer of rich dark chocolate. You can cut the bars into smaller, bite-size pieces if you like.

*makes 12*

**15 MINUTES PREPARATION TIME**
**15 MINUTES COOKING TIME**

**FOR THE SHORTBREAD BASE:**
100g (1 cup) ground almonds
75g (½ cup) arrowroot
30g (¼ cup) coconut flour
1 teaspoon vanilla extract
¼ teaspoon bicarbonate of soda
a pinch of fine sea salt
85ml (⅓ cup) maple syrup
85ml (⅓ cup) coconut oil, melted

**FOR THE DATE CARAMEL:**
12 large, soft dates, pitted
3 tablespoons almond butter
1 teaspoon vanilla extract
¼ teaspoon fine sea salt
4 tablespoons of hot water

**FOR THE CHOCOLATE LAYER:**
150g high-quality dark chocolate or
    dark chocolate chips (see page 24)
1 teaspoon coconut oil

1. Preheat the oven to 160°C/325°F/gas 3. Put all the shortbread base ingredients into a large bowl and mix well to form a smooth dough. Grab a 20 x 20cm baking tray, line it with parchment paper, then grease lightly with coconut oil. Evenly press the shortbread dough into the baking tray, then bake for 15 minutes. Let the shortbread base cool completely.

2. To make the date caramel, put all the ingredients into a food processor and whizz until it forms a smooth, sticky ball. Use the back of a spoon to press the date caramel evenly over the cooled shortbread base.

3. To make the chocolate layer, melt the chocolate and coconut oil together in a medium bowl set over a pan of simmering water, then pour the mixture over the date caramel. Set the baking tin in the fridge for 15 minutes to set the chocolate, then use a sharp knife to slice into 12 equal pieces. Store in an airtight container for up to 5 days and serve at room temperature.

# CRUNCHY NUT BANANA LOAF

Everyone loves banana cake! It's a great way to use up spotty bananas, and the nuts in my version make it high in vitamin E and protein-rich as well. Don't skip the crunchy topping – it's my favourite part. If your bananas aren't quite ripe yet, pop them into a 160°C/325°F/gas 3 oven for 30 minutes until completely blackened, to ripen them fully before using in the loaf. This freezes brilliantly once baked – just place the sliced loaf in an airtight container and keep in the freezer for up to a month.

*serves 12*

**10 MINUTES PREPARATION TIME**
**50 MINUTES COOKING TIME**

**FOR THE BANANA LOAF:**
½ teaspoon bicarbonate of soda
½ teaspoon baking powder
¼ teaspoon fine sea salt
1 teaspoon ground cinnamon
1 teaspoon vanilla extract
60ml (¼ cup) maple syrup
3 very ripe medium bananas
60ml (¼ cup) coconut oil, or melted unsalted butter
3 medium eggs
40g (⅓ cup) coconut flour
150g (1 ½ cups) ground almonds

**FOR THE CRUNCHY TOPPING:**
50g (½ cup) pecans
½ tablespoon ground cinnamon
60ml (¼ cup) coconut oil, softened but not melted
50g (½ cup) ground almonds
2 tablespoons coconut sugar or unrefined brown sugar

1. Preheat the oven to 180°C/350°F/gas 4.

2. Put all the banana cake ingredients into a food processor and whizz until smooth. Transfer the mixture to a lined and greased 450g (1lb) loaf tin.

3. Bake for 20 minutes, then remove from the oven.

4. Meanwhile, make the crunchy topping by roughly chopping the pecans and putting them into a small bowl. Add the remaining ingredients and stir well, then crumble the topping evenly over the half-baked banana cake.

5. Return to the oven for 25 to 30 minutes, until the topping is golden brown and a toothpick inserted into the centre of the cake comes out with a few crumbs attached. Let it cool for 15 minutes before removing it from the tin.

6. Enjoy the slices warm, or let the loaf cool completely and store in an airtight container, then cut slices as you need them. It'll keep in the container for up to 5 days.

# SINGLE SERVING MELT-IN-THE-MIDDLE GOOEY CHOCOLATE PUDDING

We've all had that late-night, insatiable chocolate craving, and, as it often leads to eating something you'll regret the next day, I wanted to create a single-serving healthier pudding for those times in which you just need that irresistible, indulgent hit of chocolate without the guilt. This definitely fits the bill, with a gooey puddle of chocolate flowing out of the pudding as soon as you break it open with your spoon. Although chocolate may not be the healthiest food, a brand made with unrefined sugar, raw cacao butter and cacao powder, such as the ones I've recommended on page 24, or a homemade dark chocolate actually contains some antioxidants, magnesium and iron. The fats from the coconut oil and the nutrient-rich egg add a bit of nutrition as well, but don't be fooled – this is definitely still an occasional treat!

*serves* 1

**5 MINUTES PREPARATION TIME**
**10 MINUTES COOKING TIME**

2 tablespoons coconut oil, plus
   a little for greasing
50g high-quality dark chocolate or
   dark chocolate chips (see page 24)
1 egg, beaten
1–2 tablespoons coconut sugar or
   unrefined brown sugar, depending
   on the sweetness of your chocolate
a very small pinch of fine sea salt

1. Preheat the oven to 180°C/350°F/gas 4 and lightly grease a ramekin with a bit of coconut oil.

2. In a small saucepan over low heat, melt the dark chocolate and coconut oil until smooth and silky. Remove from the heat, add the remaining ingredients and beat well with a whisk to combine.

3. Transfer the mixture to the ramekin, then bake for 10 minutes. When baked, leave to cool for a minute or so, turn the pudding out on to a plate and tuck in to your gooey, chocolatey delight!

*tip*     This recipe can easily be multiplied to serve a few and can even be made ahead – just make the mixture, pop it into the ramekins, cover them and keep in the fridge for up to 8 hours, then bake right before serving.

# FREEZER FUDGE, THREE WAYS

Freezer fudge is such an easy delight, and it's great to have a sweet bite stashed in the freezer for when you need a treat. It's hard to choose a favourite from these three — I love them all!

*makes* 16

**15 MINUTES PREPARATION TIME**

**SALTED CARAMEL:**
10 large, soft dates, pitted
60g (¼ cup) roasted almond butter
1 teaspoon vanilla bean powder
½ teaspoon flaky sea salt
1 tablespoon coconut oil
2 tablespoons maple syrup

**CHOCOLATE HAZELNUT:**
80g (½ cup) whole
  blanched hazelnuts
180g (¾ cup) roasted hazelnut
  butter (you can also make your
  own — see page 40)
60ml (¼ cup) coconut oil
60ml (¼ cup) maple syrup
35g (⅓ cup) cacao powder
1 teaspoon vanilla bean powder

**ALMOND BUTTER:**
250g (1 cup) roasted almond butter
60ml (¼ cup) coconut oil
1 teaspoon vanilla bean powder
2 tablespoons maple syrup
1 tablespoon flaked almonds,
  to decorate

1. To make the salted caramel fudge, put all the ingredients into a food processor and whizz to form a smooth ball. Press the mixture into a lined small rectangular container and freeze for at least 4 hours to set. Remove from the freezer, cut into 16 squares and sprinkle a pinch of flaky salt on top of each. Store the squares in an airtight container in the freezer. Let them sit out of the freezer for a minute or two before indulging, to let them soften just a little.

2. To make the chocolate hazelnut fudge, spread the blanched hazelnuts on a baking tray and roast for 10 minutes in a 180°C/350°F/gas 4 oven. Let them cool. Meanwhile, whizz the hazelnut butter, coconut oil, maple syrup, cacao powder and vanilla bean powder together in a food processor, until smooth. Transfer this mixture to a lined small rectangular container, sprinkle over the roasted blanched hazelnuts, and freeze for at least 4 hours to set. Remove from the freezer and cut into 16 squares. Store the squares in an airtight container in the freezer. Let them sit out of the freezer for a minute or two before indulging, to let them soften just a little.

3. To make the almond butter fudge, put all the ingredients into a food processor and whizz to form a smooth mixture. Spoon the mixture into a lined small rectangular container and freeze for at least 4 hours to set. Remove from the freezer, cut into 16 squares and place a flaked almond on top of each. Store the squares in an airtight container in the freezer. Let them sit out of the freezer for a minute or two before indulging, to let them soften just a little.

# CHOCOLATE & HAZELNUT TRUFFLES

By far the most popular recipe on my blog, these 'Ferrero Rocher' style truffles are definitely my signature recipe! They're a brilliant way to show your friends that healthy eating can be seriously delicious, and they are my go-to treat for bringing along to parties and potlucks, where they disappear within minutes. You can freeze them too if you'd like to, although I don't recommend keeping them in the house as you may well find yourself eating them all . . .

*makes 24*

**10 MINUTES PREPARATION TIME**
**+ 30 MINUTES CHILLING TIME**

125g (½ cup) roasted hazelnut butter
  (see page 40)
50g (½ cup) cacao powder
1 teaspoon vanilla bean powder
60ml (¼ cup) coconut oil
60ml (¼ cup) maple syrup
60ml (¼ cup) almond milk
24 whole blanched hazelnuts
150g (1 cup) chopped
  roasted hazelnuts
100g high-quality dark chocolate
  or dark chocolate chips
  (see page 24), melted

1. In a large bowl, mix together the hazelnut butter, cacao powder, vanilla bean powder, coconut oil, maple syrup and almond milk. Put into the freezer for 20 to 30 minutes to let the mixture firm up.

2. Meanwhile, set out the blanched whole hazelnuts, put the chopped roasted hazelnuts in a bowl and place the melted dark chocolate in another bowl. Line a baking sheet with parchment paper as well.

3. Use a teaspoon or a small ice cream scoop to take balls of the cacao-hazelnut mixture and roll between your hands quickly before placing them on the lined baking sheet. Repeat until all the mixture is used up – you should end up with about 24 balls.

4. Carefully press a whole hazelnut into each truffle from the bottom, then roll each one in the chopped roasted hazelnuts, pressing them into the truffles as you go to make sure they adhere properly. Pop the baking sheet of truffles into the freezer for 10 minutes.

5. Once chilled, dip each truffle into the melted chocolate and put back on the baking sheet. When they're all dipped, transfer the truffles to an airtight container and store in the fridge for up to 2 weeks, although I doubt they'll last that long!

# SLICE & BAKE SHORTBREAD

It's never a bad thing to have shortbread dough stashed in the freezer, ready to bake! I like to make a double batch of the recipe and bake half immediately, keeping the other half in the freezer for cookie emergencies.  A great thing about these is that you can bake just a few at a time as well. You can definitely add flavourings, too – the zest of a lemon for a zingy lemon shortbread, 1 teaspoon of ground cinnamon for a spiced shortbread, or 40g (¼ cup) of chopped dried fruit of your choice for a fruity shortbread.

*makes 24*

**10 MINUTES PREPARATION TIME**
**20 MINUTES COOKING TIME**

100g (1 cup) ground almonds
75g (½ cup) arrowroot
30g (¼ cup) coconut flour
1 teaspoon vanilla extract
¼ teaspoon bicarbonate of soda
a pinch of fine sea salt
85ml (⅓ cup) maple syrup
80ml (⅓ cup) coconut oil, melted

1.  Combine all the ingredients in a medium bowl to form a smooth, supple dough.

2.  Form the dough into a 20cm log, then roll it up in a sheet of parchment paper and twist the ends. Place in the freezer until you want to bake your cookies.

3.  When you want to bake the shortbread, preheat the oven to 160°C/325°F/gas 3 and line a baking tray. Remove the log of cookie dough from the freezer and cut into 1cm thick slices. Place on the baking tray and bake for 18 to 20 minutes, until golden brown.

# NUT & DATE ENERGY BITES

These quick energy bites are full of great ingredients, and they're brilliant for travelling, as they keep for ages. You can customize them by using your favourite nuts, adding a spoonful of cacao powder, tossing in some chocolate chips, adding a shake of cinnamon or throwing in a spoonful of chia seeds as well. The nut-free version uses shredded coconut to give a delicious chewy twist!

*makes 12*

**10 MINUTES PREPARATION TIME**

80g (½ cup) roasted nuts
   (I like almonds or pecans best),
   or raw shredded coconut
   for a nut-free version
10 soft and squishy dates, pitted
1 tablespoon nut butter, any kind
   (omit for nut-free version)
1 teaspoon coconut oil
½ teaspoon vanilla bean powder

**OPTIONAL TOPPINGS:**
shredded coconut, cacao powder

1. Put all the ingredients into a food processor and whizz for 2 to 3 minutes, until the mixture comes together. You might have to scrape the processor down a few times along the way!

2. Roll the mixture into small balls in the palm of your hands, then roll the balls in shredded coconut or cacao powder. You can also leave them plain.

3. Pop them into an airtight container and place them in the fridge, where they'll keep for up to 2 weeks.

# CINNAMON MAPLE GLAZED WALNUTS

These are dangerously addictive! They always disappear very quickly in my house, as everyone loves the crunchy spiced coating. You can use pecans instead for a change.

*makes 150g*

**15 MINUTES PREPARATION TIME**

1 tablespoon coconut oil
80ml (¹/₃ cup) maple syrup
2 teaspoons vanilla extract
1 teaspoon ground cinnamon
225g (1 ½ cups) raw walnuts

1. Combine the coconut oil, maple syrup, vanilla extract and cinnamon in a small saucepan over a medium heat and simmer for 5 minutes, whisking constantly. Add the walnuts and continue to stir over a medium heat for a few minutes with a spatula or wooden spoon until the mixture has thickened and clings to the walnuts – they should be coated with a thick, shiny sauce.

2. Transfer the walnuts to a lined baking tray and let them cool for 30 minutes, so that the glaze sets. Store in an airtight container at room temperature for up to 2 weeks.

# SALTY & SPICY PUMPKIN SEEDS

A handful of these crunchy roasted seeds makes a delicious and filling snack. As well as vitamin E, pumpkin seeds provide iron, magnesium and zinc. You can adjust the cayenne pepper to your taste if you wish!

*makes 300g*

**15 MINUTES PREPARATION TIME**

300g (2 cups) pumpkin seeds
1 tablespoon extra virgin olive oil
½ teaspoon fine sea salt
¼ teaspoon cayenne pepper
½ teaspoon garlic powder

1. Preheat the oven to 180°C/350°F/gas 4 and line a baking tray with parchment paper.

2. Combine all the ingredients in a small bowl until the seeds are evenly coated. Transfer to the baking tray and roast for 15 minutes, until they're fragrant. Let the pumpkin seeds cool for at least 15 minutes, then enjoy or store in an airtight container for up to 2 weeks.

# RAW CACAO COCONUT MACAROONS

With three varieties of coconut, these macaroons certainly deliver on taste!
They're very easy to whip up and even easier to shovel down.

*makes 24*

**15 MINUTES PREPARATION TIME**
**20 MINUTES CHILLING TIME**

160g (2 cups) unsweetened
   desiccated coconut
2 tablespoons full-fat tinned
   coconut milk
80ml ($1/3$ cup) coconut oil
25g (¼ cup) cacao powder
60ml (¼ cup) maple syrup
½ teaspoon vanilla bean powder
50g high-quality dark chocolate or
   dark chocolate chips (see page 24)

1. Put all the ingredients except the dark chocolate into a
bowl and stir very well to combine. Use a small ice cream
scoop, a melon baller or a tablespoon to scoop the mixture
on to a lined baking tray or wire rack. Repeat until all the
mixture is used up, then place the tray in the fridge for 20
minutes for the macaroons to set.

2. Melt the dark chocolate, then drizzle it evenly over the
macaroons. Store in an airtight container in the fridge for up
to a week.

# ALMOND BUTTER STUFFED DATES

This is a sticky, squishy snack that will satisfy even the strongest of sweet cravings!
Don't let the simplicity of the recipe fool you – these are a really delicious little treat.
Sprinkle with flaked almonds to dress them up a bit if you want!

*serves* 1

**5 MINUTES PREPARATION TIME**

2 large, soft dates
2 teaspoons almond butter

1. Open up the dates and remove the stones, then spoon
1 teaspoon of almond butter into each date. Enjoy!

# SERIOUSLY DECADENT DESSERTS

Much as I love a good salad, I definitely have a weakness for desserts! There's no reason to think that you can't enjoy a slice of chocolate torte or a warm berry crumble with a big scoop of coconut ice cream when you're eating a wholesome, unprocessed diet, but remember that just because they're healthier doesn't mean you can eat them at every meal, sadly! These recipes range from simple ice lollies you can whip up in minutes to a show-stopping mango & lime tart fit for any celebration, and I promise they taste even better than their sugar-stuffed traditional counterparts.

# DEATH-BY-CHOCOLATE PISTACHIO DARK CHOCOLATE TORTE WITH BERRY COULIS

This cake is truly the epitome of indulgence! Dark and squidgy, with a fruit coulis on the side to lighten things up a little, it's made with just five ingredients including plenty of healthy fats and uses unrefined coconut sugar to sweeten. The pistachios are nutrient-dense and high in potassium and vitamin K, but if you can't find any unsalted raw shelled ones, substitute 100g (1 cup) of ground almonds instead and just fold them straight into the whipped eggs and sugar mixture.

*serves* 16

10 MINUTES PREPARATION TIME
35 MINUTES COOKING TIME
2 HOURS COOLING TIME

**FOR THE TORTE:**
200ml (1 cup) coconut oil, or melted
  unsalted butter
200g high-quality dark chocolate or
  dark chocolate chips (see page 24)
150g (1 cup) unsalted raw
  shelled pistachios
5 medium eggs
160g (1⅓ cups) coconut sugar or
  unrefined brown sugar

**FOR THE COULIS:**
200g mixed berries, frozen or fresh
1 tablespoon maple syrup

**TO SERVE (OPTIONAL):**
coconut whipped cream (see page
  257) and chopped pistachios

1. Preheat the oven to 180°C/350°F/gas 4, then grease a 20cm round cake tin with a little coconut oil and line it with parchment paper.

2. Place the coconut oil and dark chocolate in a heatproof bowl and place over a small saucepan filled a quarter of the way up with very hot water, ensuring that the bottom of the bowl is not touching the water. Heat gently until the coconut oil and chocolate are completely melted, then remove the bowl and set aside.

3. Meanwhile, place the raw shelled pistachios in a food processor and whizz until very fine. Sieve the ground pistachios into a bowl and discard any large chunks.

4. Put the eggs and the coconut sugar into a large bowl and whisk with a handheld mixer for 5 to 6 minutes, until light in colour, fluffy and thick. Gently fold in the sieved ground pistachios and the melted chocolate mixture. Once evenly combined, transfer the mixture to the greased and lined cake tin and smooth the top with a spatula. ➤

5. Bake for 35 minutes, then remove from the oven and cool. Carefully remove the cake from the tin, transfer to a plate and place in the fridge for 2 hours.

6. Either serve immediately in small slices (it's rich!) with a generous amount of warm coulis, a dollop of coconut whipped cream and a sprinkle of chopped pistachios, or place the cake in an airtight container, where you can store it at room temperature for up to a day or frozen for up to a month before serving.

7. Right before serving, make the coulis by putting the berries and maple syrup into a small saucepan over medium heat and warming for 5 minutes, until bubbling. Pour a generous amount of coulis over the cake and enjoy!

# CINNAMON STEWED PEACHES
# WITH PECAN CRUNCH

One of the most disappointing things in the summer is a rock-hard, unripe peach,
but this is the perfect way to use them up and turn them into soft, stewed
cinnamon-spiced deliciousness! With a crunchy pecan crunch on the side,
it's the perfect quick and easy summery dessert.

*serves 4*

**15 MINUTES PREPARATION TIME**
**20 MINUTES COOKING TIME**

**FOR THE PEACHES:**
1 tablespoon coconut oil
1 tablespoon maple syrup
1 teaspoon ground cinnamon
4 peaches, peeled, pitted and
    cut into quarters
60ml (¼ cup) water

**FOR THE PECAN CRUNCH:**
150g (1 cup) raw pecans,
    finely chopped
35g (½ cup) unsweetened
    desiccated coconut
1 tablespoon coconut oil
1 tablespoon maple syrup
1 teaspoon ground cinnamon

1. Preheat the oven to 160°C/325°F/gas 3 and line a
baking sheet with parchment paper.

2. To make the pecan crunch, stir the finely chopped
pecans, desiccated coconut, coconut oil, maple syrup and
cinnamon together in a bowl. Spread the mixture over
the lined baking sheet and bake for 12 to 15 minutes, until
golden brown.

3. Meanwhile, heat the coconut oil, maple syrup and
cinnamon in a frying pan over medium heat, stirring well,
until bubbling. Add the sliced peaches and toss them in the
syrup to coat them. Stir in the water, then cover the pan
and cook for 8 to 10 minutes, until the peaches are soft and
the sauce has thickened.

4. Serve the stewed peaches with a small handful of the
pecan crunch.

# SALTED CARAMEL COCONUT
# ICE CREAM PARFAITS

This is by quite a far stretch the most indulgent recipe in the book – scoops of luscious coconut milk ice cream with a decadent date caramel swirl, all topped with coconut whipped cream and a cheeky drizzle of salted caramel sauce. It's very rich, which is why you only need a small portion, and it's a great thing to share with friends. While I know many people are a fan of the very popular one-ingredient frozen banana 'ice cream', frozen bananas are actually very high in sugar, so I've used full-fat coconut milk here as the ice cream base.

*serves 8*

**15 MINUTES PREPARATION TIME
+ 2 HOURS FREEZING TIME**

**FOR THE ICE CREAM:**
1 x 400ml tin of full-fat coconut milk
6 soft, squidgy dates, pitted
35g (¼ cup) coconut sugar or
   unrefined brown sugar
1 teaspoon vanilla bean powder
½ teaspoon fine sea salt

**FOR THE CARAMEL SWIRL:**
10 soft, squidgy dates, pitted
60ml (¼ cup) boiling water
½ teaspoon fine sea salt

**TO SERVE:**
coconut whipped cream (see
   page 256)
salted caramel sauce (see page 260)

1. Make the ice cream first by placing all the ingredients in a blender and whizzing until completely smooth. Place the mixture in a bowl, then pop in the fridge for about an hour, until chilled. Transfer to an ice cream maker and churn according to manufacturer's instructions.

2. Meanwhile, make the caramel swirl by whizzing all the ingredients in a food processor for 2 to 3 minutes, scraping down the sides quite often, until you have a smooth caramel mixture.

3. Once the ice cream is done churning, transfer it to an airtight container, then use a spoon to swirl the date caramel throughout. Pop into the freezer for at least 2 hours to firm up – it'll keep for up to a month.

4. About 10 minutes before serving, get the ice cream out of the freezer to let it soften before you scoop it. Serve the ice cream with dollops of coconut whipped cream and drizzles of salted caramel sauce. Enjoy!

If you haven't got an ice cream maker, pop the chilled ice cream mixture into an airtight container and freeze for 3 to 4 hours, stirring very well every 20 minutes or so, until you have a soft ice cream, then let it firm up for a further 2 hours before serving. Remember to leave it out of the freezer for 10 minutes to soften before you try to scoop it!

# BLUEBERRY & ALMOND CRUMBLE SLICE

Inspired by a day of blueberry picking in the forest one summer, after which I ended up with bags upon bags of fresh berries to use up, this blueberry crumble slice is comforting and nourishing, with nutrient-rich blueberries bursting their way through a delicious crumble topping. You can definitely use other summer berries here as well, although blueberries are particularly bubbly and juicy and make for a brilliant treat.

*makes* 16

10 MINUTES PREPARATION TIME
30 MINUTES COOKING TIME

FOR THE BASE:
200g (2 cups) ground almonds
30g (¼ cup) coconut flour
75g (½ cup) arrowroot
140g (1 cup) coconut sugar or
  unrefined brown sugar
125ml (½ cup) coconut oil, melted
60ml (¼ cup) full-fat tinned
  coconut milk
1 teaspoon vanilla extract
½ teaspoon bicarbonate of soda
½ teaspoon fine sea salt

FOR THE FILLING:
400g fresh or frozen blueberries
1 tablespoon arrowroot
1 tablespoon lemon juice
50g (½ cup) flaked almonds

1. Preheat your oven to 180°C/350°F/gas 4 and line a square baking tray with parchment paper.

2. In a large bowl, combine the ground almonds, coconut flour, arrowroot, coconut sugar, coconut oil, coconut milk, vanilla extract, bicarbonate of soda and sea salt to form a crumbly dough.

3. Take a handful (about half a cup) of this dough mixture and set it aside in a small bowl to use later. Press the remaining dough into the lined baking tray to form a crust. Bake the crust for 12 minutes, until slightly browned.

4. Meanwhile, pop the blueberries, arrowroot and lemon juice into a saucepan over a medium heat and stew, stirring constantly, for about 5 minutes, until the blueberries burst and form a thick sauce.

5. Once the crust has cooked, spread the blueberry sauce mixture on top. Grab the mixture you set aside earlier and add the flaked almonds to this, then mix together gently with your hands to form a crumble topping. Sprinkle this topping over the blueberries and bake the whole thing for 20 minutes, until golden brown.

6. Cool, then cut into 16 pieces with a sharp knife and carefully lift them out of the baking tray with a spatula. It's quite fragile, so it may crumble a little, but don't worry – it will still taste great!

# POMEGRANATE, ORANGE & GOJI BERRY MINCE PIES

I was never a huge fan of mince pies until I tried my hand at making them a little healthier, and now I can't imagine the festive season without these delicious little almond-crusted pies filled with a sweet, juicy pomegranate, orange and goji berry mincemeat! You'll have some mincemeat left over, so pop it into a sealed glass jar and keep it in the fridge for up to a week – either use it to make some more mince pies or enjoy it as a festive pancake topping!

*makes 6*

**20 MINUTES PREPARATION TIME**
**25 MINUTES COOKING TIME**

**FOR THE MINCEMEAT:**
6 tablespoons coconut sugar or
   unrefined brown sugar
60ml (¼ cup) pomegranate juice
2 medium apples, grated
40g (¼ cup) goji berries (use raisins
   instead if you don't have them)
1 teaspoon ground cinnamon
zest and juice of 1 orange
½ teaspoon ground nutmeg
½ teaspoon ground cloves

**FOR THE PASTRY:**
100g (1 cup) ground almonds
2 tablespoons coconut flour
50g (⅓ cup) arrowroot
60ml (¼ cup) maple syrup
60ml (¼ cup) coconut oil, melted
1 teaspoon vanilla extract
coconut sugar or unrefined brown
   sugar, for sprinkling on top

1. To make the mincemeat, mix all the ingredients in a saucepan over a medium heat for about 10 minutes, until bubbling, then remove from the heat and set aside.

2. Once you're ready to make the pies, preheat the oven to 180°C/350°F/gas 4 and grease a shallow bun tray with a little coconut oil. In a large bowl, combine the pastry ingredients until they form a smooth dough, then wrap or cover the dough and pop it into the fridge for 15 minutes to firm up.

3. Working quickly, roll the dough out between two sheets of parchment paper, both dusted with a little arrowroot, to about ½cm thick. Use a circular cookie cutter to cut out 6 pastry bases. Use a star-shaped cookie cutter to cut out 6 stars for the top, and set aside. Using a spatula, carefully transfer the pastry bases to the bun tray and very carefully push the pastry down into the tin. Repeat for the remaining 5 bases, then bake for 7 to 8 minutes.

4. Add a tablespoon of the mincemeat to each base, top with a pastry star and sprinkle with a little coconut sugar, then pop them back into the oven for 15 minutes, until golden brown. Let them cool for 15 minutes, until slightly firmed up, and enjoy warm.

# CHOCOLATE COCONUT ICE LOLLIES

These creamy, chocolatey ice lollies are drizzled with a coating of dark chocolate to make them even more indulgent. They only take a few minutes to make but are well worth the effort, and with only about half a date's worth of sugar per serving, they're very low in sugar as well.

*makes 8*

**15 MINUTES PREPARATION TIME**
**4 HOURS FREEZING TIME**

1 x 400ml tin of full-fat coconut milk
180ml (¾ cup) almond milk
½ teaspoon vanilla bean powder
5 dates, pitted
35g (⅓ cup) cacao powder
100g high-quality dark chocolate or
   dark chocolate chips (see page 24)

**OPTIONAL:**
Coconut flakes or chopped nuts
   to decorate

1. Put the coconut milk, almond milk, vanilla bean powder, dates and cacao powder into a blender and blend until smooth.

2. Divide the mixture evenly between 8 lollipop moulds. If you don't have any of these, you can pour the mixture into disposable paper cups and insert a lolly stick in the middle. Let them freeze for at least 4 hours.

3. Right before serving, melt the dark chocolate (if using it) to decorate the ice lollies. Remove the ice lollies from their moulds and drizzle with melted chocolate, then sprinkle with coconut flakes or chopped nuts. Let them sit for a minute or two to soften before enjoying! You can store any leftovers in an airtight container in the freezer for up to a month.

# PINEAPPLE CARROT CAKE WITH PASSIONFRUIT COCONUT FROSTING

Made with fresh pineapple and nutrient-dense ground almonds, this tropical cake is absolutely delicious on its own, but even better when slathered with passionfruit coconut cream frosting. It's important to let the coconut sugar syrup cool completely before adding it to the whipped coconut cream or you'll end up with a runny mess!

*serves* 12

15 MINUTES PREPARATION TIME
30 MINUTES COOKING TIME
+ 2 HOURS COOLING TIME

**FOR THE CAKE:**
2 eggs, beaten
70g (½ cup) coconut sugar or
   unrefined brown sugar
2 tablespoons coconut oil
200g (2 cups) ground almonds
½ teaspoon bicarbonate of soda
½ teaspoon ground cinnamon
2 medium carrots, grated
100g (½ cup) fresh pineapple chunks,
   very finely chopped
40g (¼ cup) raisins
20g (¼ cup) unsweetened
   shredded coconut

**FOR THE FROSTING:**
70g (½ cup) coconut sugar or
   unrefined brown sugar
1 x 400ml tin of full-fat coconut milk,
   left in the fridge for at
   least 24 hours
3 passionfruit, pulp scooped out

**TO DECORATE:**
passionfruit pulp, fresh pineapple
   chunks and flaked almonds

1. Preheat the oven to 160°C/325°F, then line a 20cm loose-based cake tin with parchment paper and lightly grease with a bit of coconut oil.

2. Start by making the coconut sugar syrup for the frosting, as it'll need time to cool. Pop the coconut sugar into a saucepan with 2 tablespoons of water over a medium heat and whisk constantly for 2 minutes until it dissolves into a thick syrup. Take it off the heat as soon as it has dissolved. Transfer to a bowl and leave at room temperature for 2 hours.

3. To make the cake, beat the eggs, coconut sugar, coconut oil, ground almonds, bicarbonate of soda and ground cinnamon to form a light batter. Stir in the carrots, pineapple, raisins and shredded coconut. Transfer into the lined tin and smooth with the back of a spoon. Bake for 30 minutes, until golden and a toothpick comes out cleanly from the middle, then let it cool completely.

4. Once the cake is cooled, continue making the frosting. Turn the chilled tin of coconut milk upside down, open, then pour the watery layer into a bowl (use this later for a smoothie). Scoop the creamy layer into a big bowl, then whisk until thick and fluffy. Gently stir the cooled coconut sugar syrup into the coconut cream to form a thick frosting. Put the passionfruit pulp through a sieve and add the juice to the coconut cream mixture.

5. Right before serving, spread the cake generously with the coconut cream mixture and decorate.

# RAINBOW COCONUT WATER ICE LOLLIES

Made with just fresh fruit and a splash of refreshing coconut water, these rainbow popsicles are definitely worth the time and effort! Using fruit purées packs them with flavour, fibre and nutrition, so they're a much better option than the usual sugar-loaded, artificially coloured ice lollies. Use watermelon instead of strawberries, oranges instead of mango or blackberries instead of blueberries if you wish, and if you can't find any coconut water, don't worry about it – they'll taste just as good without.

*makes 8*

**15 MINUTES PREPARATION TIME
+ 3 HOURS FREEZING TIME**

125ml (½ cup) coconut water
a big handful (about 150g) of fresh
   strawberries, hulled
1 mango, peeled and stone removed
   (see page 228)
a big handful (about 150g) of fresh
   pineapple chunks
2 kiwis, peeled
a big handful (about 75g) of
   fresh blueberries

1. Whizz the strawberries with 1½ tablespoons of coconut water using a stick blender to form a smooth purée, then fill 8 ice lolly moulds one-fifth of the way up with the strawberry purée. Pop into the freezer for 15 minutes to set.

2. Rinse the immersion blender, then whizz the mango flesh with another 1½ tablespoons of coconut water to form a purée. Add a layer of mango on top of the strawberry layer and put back into the freezer to set for another 15 minutes.

3. Repeat this process, rinsing out the blender before you make each purée of fruit and coconut water and letting each layer set for 15 minutes in the freezer before adding the next one, until all the different fruit purées are used up. Make sure you layer them in the right order to get the rainbow effect: strawberries, mango, pineapple, kiwi and blueberries. Once all the layers are done, put the ice lollies into the freezer for an hour to let them fully set before enjoying!

*tip*

Use any leftover fruit purée in smoothies.

# MANGO LIME TART

Thanks to the gorgeous bright colours of the mango and lime along with a little decorating trick, this tart looks very impressive, but it takes hardly any time to make – I promise! The simple almond crust filled with a rich, creamy coconut, mango and lime filling and decorated with thinly sliced mango doesn't just look stunning but tastes incredible as well … a true show-stopper!

*serves 10*

**20 MINUTES PREPARATION TIME**
**15 MINUTES BAKING TIME**

**FOR THE CRUST:**
100g (1 cup) ground almonds
40g (¼ cup) arrowroot
2 tablespoons coconut flour
60ml (¼ cup) coconut oil, melted
60ml (¼ cup) maple syrup
1 teaspoon vanilla extract

**FOR THE FILLING:**
1 x 400ml tin of full-fat coconut
  milk, left in the fridge for at
  least 24 hours
the zest and juice of 1 lime
2 tablespoons maple syrup
2 mangoes, peeled

**TO DECORATE:**
2 mangoes
the zest of 1 lime

1. Preheat the oven to 180°C/350°F/gas 4.

2. Make the crust by whizzing together all the ingredients in a food processor until completely combined, then press the crust into a loose-bottomed tin lined with parchment paper and bake for 15 minutes, until golden brown. Take out of the oven and leave for at least 30 minutes, until completely cool.

3. Meanwhile, open the tin of coconut milk and pour the watery layer at the top into a bowl to use for smoothies later on. Use a spoon to transfer the thick, creamy layer at the bottom to the food processor, then add the lime zest, lime juice and maple syrup. Take your peeled mangoes and hold them upright on a chopping board, then slice down one side of each mango with a sharp knife, cutting as closely as possible to the big stone in the middle – from each mango, you should end up with two big pieces of mango flesh sliced from each side of the flat stone in the middle. Transfer the flesh to the food processor as well, then whizz everything together for 2 to 3 minutes, until completely smooth and thick. Pour this mixture into the crust and put into the fridge for an hour to set.

4. Prepare the mangoes for the decoration in the same way as described above, then slice the mango 'sides' thinly to form slices. Start with the longer slices of mango and use them to line the edge of the tart, then work your way to the middle of the tart in the same way. Once you're at the middle, roll up a mango slice and pop it right in the centre to finish your design. Scatter the lime zest on top, then serve immediately or keep in the fridge for a few hours before serving.

# FANCY FRUIT SALAD

Everyone loves a fruit salad – it's the perfect healthy dessert option and you can use any fruit you want! This fancied-up version is tossed with a 'dressing' made from freshly squeezed orange juice, passion fruit pulp and lots of mint for an extra flavour boost. You can get creative and use cookie cutters to cut out shapes from the fruit, or even serve the fruit salad in a scooped-out pineapple half!

*serves 8*

**20 MINUTES PREPARATION TIME**

A selection of your favourite fruit –
apples, pears, melon, mango,
oranges, pineapple, berries,
pomegranate, banana, peaches,
plums or grapes are all great

**FOR THE DRESSING:**
two passionfruit, cut in half and
insides scooped out
the juice of 1 large orange
a big handful of mint, chopped

1. Chop up all your fruit into bite-sized pieces and pop into a big bowl.

2. In a smaller bowl, mix together the orange juice, mint and passionfruit pulp until well combined, then pour this over the chopped-up fruit and toss to combine.

3. Serve the fruit salad plain or with a dollop of coconut yoghurt and garnish with a sprig of mint if you want!

# SUMMER BERRY CRUMBLE WITH CHAI COCONUT ICE CREAM

Who doesn't love a crumble? This version, crammed with fresh summer berries and adorned with a flaky topping made from almonds, a bit of coconut oil and a sprinkling of unrefined coconut sugar, is absolutely delicious with a generous scoop of the creamy spiced coconut milk ice cream. The crumble can be made in individual little ramekins or ovenproof mugs if you wish – just reduce the cooking time to about 15 minutes. If you have any leftover crumble topping (and manage not to scoff it all down!), you can pop it into an airtight container in the fridge and use it within 2 days.

*serves 6*

---

15 MINUTES PREPARATION TIME
30 MINUTES COOKING TIME
+ 2 HOURS FREEZING TIME

**FOR THE CRUMBLE:**
400g mixture of fresh strawberries, blueberries and raspberries
100g (1 cup) ground almonds
25g (¼ cup) flaked almonds
60ml (¼ cup) coconut oil
35g (¼ cup) coconut sugar or unrefined brown sugar

**FOR THE CHAI ICE CREAM:**
1 x 400ml tin of full-fat coconut milk
6 soft, squidgy dates, pitted
1 teaspoon vanilla bean powder
1 teaspoon ground cinnamon
¼ teaspoon ground nutmeg
¼ teaspoon ground cloves
¼ teaspoon ground cardamom

1. Make the ice cream first by placing all the ingredients in a blender and whizzing until completely smooth. Place the mixture in a bowl, then pop in the fridge for about an hour until chilled. Transfer to an ice cream maker and churn according to the manufacturer's instructions. Transfer the ice cream to an airtight container and pop into the freezer for at least 2 hours to firm up – it'll keep for up to a month.

2. To make the crumble, preheat the oven to 180°C/350°F/gas 4. Slice the strawberries, then pop all the berries into a medium baking dish. In a separate bowl, use your fingers to gently combine the remaining ingredients to form a crumbly mixture. Sprinkle this mixture over the berries, then bake for 20 to 25 minutes, until the topping is golden brown and the berries are juicy and bursting. About halfway through cooking, remove the coconut ice cream from the freezer to allow it to soften a little so that it's easily scoopable!

3. Once cooked, let the crumble cool just slightly, then serve with scoops of the chai coconut ice cream.

---

*tip*

If you haven't got an ice cream maker, pop the chilled ice cream mixture into an airtight container and freeze for 3 to 4 hours, stirring very well every 20 minutes or so, until you have a soft ice cream, then let it firm up for a further 2 hours before serving. Remember to leave it out of the freezer for 10 minutes to let it soften before you try to scoop it!

---

# CHOCOLATE-DIPPED ALMOND
# ICE CREAM BARS

One of the very first things I ever posted on my blog was a recipe for chocolate cashew ice cream bars, so I gave that recipe a makeover and turned it into these chocolate-dipped 'Snickers' ice cream bars! With four layers all dipped in silky dark chocolate, this really is a decadent dessert. Use my chocolate cacao ice cream (see page 222) instead of the ice cream recipe below to make a double chocolate version if you want!

## makes 12

**30 MINUTES PREPARATION TIME
+ 2½ HOURS FREEZING TIME**

**FOR THE ICE CREAM LAYER:**
1 x 400ml tin of full-fat coconut milk
6 soft, squidgy dates, pitted
35g (¼ cup) coconut sugar or
   unrefined brown sugar
1 teaspoon vanilla bean powder
½ teaspoon fine sea salt

**FOR THE CARAMEL LAYER:**
10 soft, squidgy dates, pitted
100ml (⅓ cup) boiling water
½ teaspoon fine sea salt

**FOR THE SALTED ALMOND LAYER:**
125g (½ cup) roasted almond butter
2 tablespoons coconut oil
2 tablespoons maple syrup
40g (¼ cup) roasted almonds,
   roughly chopped
½ teaspoon flaky sea salt

**FOR THE CHOCOLATE DIP:**
100g high-quality dark chocolate or
   dark chocolate chips (see page 24)
1 teaspoon coconut oil

1. Put all the ice cream ingredients into a blender and whizz for a minute, until completely smooth and combined. Transfer the mixture to a shallow rectangular container lined with parchment paper, then pop into the freezer for 2 hours.

2. Meanwhile, make the caramel layer by putting all the ingredients into a food processor and whizzing to make a smooth, thick caramel. You might need to add a few more spoonfuls of boiling water to make a smooth paste.

3. Make the almond layer by stirring together all the ingredients in a bowl.

4. Remove the frozen ice cream base from the freezer, then take your date caramel and use a knife to spread it over the ice cream layer. Spoon the almond layer on top and spread evenly over the caramel layer. Transfer the container to the freezer for 30 minutes to allow everything to harden. Meanwhile, melt the chocolate and coconut oil in a small saucepan over a very low heat until smooth and silky.

6. Once the layers have set, use a sharp knife to slice the slab into 12 pieces to form individual ice cream bars. Dip the bars into the melted chocolate, sprinkle with a little flaky salt, then enjoy immediately or pop them into an airtight container and keep in the freezer for up to a month. Let them sit out at room temperature for a few minutes before enjoying if you do this, though.

# RUSTIC RHUBARB & APPLE GALETTE WITH ALMOND CRUST

A galette is a French free-form, rustic pie – essentially it's a lot less fussy than a proper pie and is supposed to look a little homemade, so you don't have to worry about making it look perfect. With the slight tang of rhubarb and the sweetness of apples atop an almond-flavoured crust, it's an easy yet impressive dessert.

*serves 12*

**20 MINUTES PREPARATION TIME**
**30 MINUTES COOKING TIME**

**FOR THE CRUST:**
100g (1 cup) ground almonds
50g ($^1/_3$ cup) arrowroot
2 tablespoons coconut flour
60ml (¼ cup) coconut oil, melted
60ml (¼ cup) maple syrup
1 teaspoon vanilla extract
¼ teaspoon fine sea salt
½ teaspoon bicarbonate of soda

**FOR THE FILLING:**
2 stalks of rhubarb, ends sliced off
   and cut into 2½cm pieces
1 apple, peeled, cored and cut into
   ½cm thick slices
½ teaspoon vanilla bean powder
2 tablespoons arrowroot
45g (¼ cup) coconut sugar or
   unrefined brown sugar

**TO SPRINKLE OVER:**
coconut sugar or unrefined
   brown sugar
flaked almonds

1. Preheat the oven to 160°C/325°F/gas 3.

2. Combine all the crust ingredients in a large bowl to form a soft, pliable dough. Cover the dough and freeze for 10 minutes to firm up a little.

3. While the dough chills, make the filling by combining all the ingredients in a small bowl until evenly mixed.

4. Remove the dough from the freezer, knead until pliable, then roll it out between two sheets of parchment paper dusted with a little arrowroot. Roll to an approximate circle until it is about ½cm thick.

5. Remove the top sheet of parchment paper, then transfer the dough on the bottom sheet of parchment paper to a baking sheet. Add the filling to the middle of the dough and spread it out, leaving about 5cm uncovered around the edges.

6. Fold the edges of the dough over the rhubarb and apple filling to form a crust. Sprinkle a little coconut sugar and a handful of flaked almonds over the crust, then bake for 25 to 30 minutes, until the crust is golden brown and the filling is soft and juicy. Allow to cool, then slice with a sharp knife and carefully transfer small wedges to plates using a spatula. Enjoy!

# LEMON ZEST, BLUEBERRY & ALMOND FRENCH MADELEINES

Essentially just posh little cakes, these dainty little madeleines are super-easy to make but look very impressive and are brilliant with a big mug of herbal tea. I've added lemon and antioxidant-rich fresh blueberries for a delicious twist. If you haven't got a madeleine mould (you can find them in most big supermarkets), turn them into mini muffins instead, using the tip below.

*makes 24*

**15 MINUTES PREPARATION TIME**
**15 MINUTES COOKING TIME**

150g (1½ cups) ground almonds
1 teaspoon baking powder
3 tablespoons coconut flour
3 tablespoons arrowroot
3 eggs
125ml (½ cup) maple syrup
125ml (½ cup) coconut oil, plus a
    little for greasing
1 tablespoon vanilla extract
60ml (¼ cup) full-fat tinned
    coconut milk
the zest and juice of 1
    unwaxed lemon
a big handful (about 75g) of
    fresh blueberries

1. Preheat the oven to 180°C/350°F/gas 4.

2. In a big bowl, whisk together the ground almonds, baking powder, coconut flour and arrowroot until combined, then stir in the eggs, maple syrup, coconut oil, vanilla extract, coconut milk, lemon zest and juice to form a smooth batter. Gently fold in the fresh blueberries.

3. Grease a madeleine mould with a little bit of coconut oil, then dollop scoops of the batter into the mould and spread out with the back of a spoon. Repeat until all the batter is used up, then bake for 12 to 15 minutes, until the madeleines are golden brown. Leave to cool slightly before enjoying with a cup of tea, and store any leftovers in an airtight container in the freezer for up to a month.

*tip* If you haven't got a madeleine mould, you can easily turn these into mini muffins by dolloping the batter into a lightly greased mini muffin tray lined with mini parchment paper baking cups and baking them for about 10 minutes instead.

# SAUCES, DRESSINGS, TOPPINGS & TITBITS

These are my staples – the things you'll always find in my fridge, the ones I've always got on hand and the little things that can turn a boring meal into something great. From a fiery, spicy carrot curry sauce to my favourite seeded crackers, these recipes are a quick and easy way to bump up flavour. You'll also find a tutorial about how to make your own vanilla extract, simple sweet and savoury dips, and dessert basics like coconut whipped cream and raw chocolate ganache.

# CARROT CORIANDER CURRY SAUCE

This is a life-saver on those nights where you don't have much time to be in the kitchen – throw everything into a pot, let it simmer away, and pour it over some sautéed chicken strips or a plateful of steamed veg for a very quick but delicious dinner. The natural sweetness of the carrots contrasts beautifully with the fragrant curry powder and the spicy coriander.

*makes 500ml or 2 cups*

**10 MINUTES PREPARATION TIME**
**30 MINUTES COOKING TIME**

3 carrots, peeled and sliced
1 clove of garlic, finely chopped
a 2.5cm piece of lemongrass,
   finely chopped
250ml (1 cup) boiling water
1 homemade chicken stock cube
   (see pages 76–79)
250ml (1 cup) full-fat tinned
   coconut milk
1 tablespoon coconut aminos
   (see page 23) or gluten-free tamari
2 heaped teaspoons curry powder
½ teaspoon fine sea salt
a handful of fresh coriander

1. Put all the ingredients except the coriander into a small saucepan over a medium heat.

2. Simmer for 30 minutes, then remove the pan from the heat.

3. Add the coriander, then use a stick blender to blend until smooth and creamy. Keep leftovers in a sealed jar in the fridge for up to a week.

# FRUIT & HERB INFUSED WATER

Colourful, fruity and delicious, these fruit and herb infused waters are a great way to start drinking more water. These are a few of my favourite combinations, but try making your own! You can also use frozen fruit, which is often cheaper than fresh fruit and tastes just as good.

*makes 250ml or 1 cup*

**5 MINUTES PREPARATION TIME**

**FOR THE CUCUMBER-LEMON -BLUEBERRY:**
1 litre water (still or sparkling)
1 lemon, cut into slices
a few handfuls of blueberries
½ a cucumber, peeled into strips

**FOR THE ORANGE-STRAWBERRY -MINT:**
1 litre water (still or sparkling)
a big handful of fresh mint,
  roughly chopped
1 orange, cut into slices
a handful of strawberries, halved

**FOR THE PINEAPPLE-POMEGRANATE -MANGO:**
1 litre water (still or sparkling)
1 mango, cubed or sliced
a handful of pomegranate seeds
a handful of chopped pineapple

1. Add the fruit to the bottom of a tall glass jar, then use one end of a rolling pin to smash it up a little (this releases the flavour). Add the herbs if using, then fill up to the top of the container with water. Keep in the fridge for 1 to 2 days (and if you drink all the water before that, you can refill your jar with water as well!).

# LEMON GARLIC VINAIGRETTE

I love this bright yet very tasty dressing – it's brilliant on all sorts of greens and salads!

*makes 60ml or 1/4 cup*

**5 MINUTES PREPARATION TIME**

60ml (¼ cup) extra virgin olive oil
juice of ½ a lemon (about 1 tablespoon)
1 teaspoon garlic powder
¼ teaspoon fine sea salt
½ teaspoon smooth Dijon mustard
½ teaspoon of freshly ground black pepper

1. Put all the ingredients into a small screwtop jar, pop the lid on, then shake. Store in the fridge.

# ORANGE VINAIGRETTE

Zingy and fruity, this vinaigrette adds a lovely summery touch to any salad!

*makes 60ml or 1/2 cup*

**10 MINUTES PREPARATION TIME**

60ml (½ cup) extra virgin olive oil
zest and juice of 2 unwaxed oranges
1 teaspoon Dijon mustard
1 teaspoon honey
½ teaspoon fine sea salt
½ teaspoon freshly ground black pepper

1. Put all the ingredients into a small screwtop jar, pop the lid on, then shake. Store in the fridge.

# CREAMY COCONUT BALSAMIC DRESSING

This dressing provides a rich, creamy alternative to vinaigrettes. It's particularly good on peppery greens like rocket and watercress, as the slight hint of coconut counterbalances their sharpness.

*makes 250ml or 1 cup*

**10 MINUTES PREPARATION TIME**

60ml (¼ cup) full-fat tinned coconut milk
170ml (⅔ cup) extra virgin olive oil
85ml (⅓ cup ) high-quality balsamic vinegar
½ teaspoon fine sea salt
½ teaspoon freshly ground black pepper

1. Put all the ingredients into a screwtop jar, pop the lid on, then shake very well to combine. Store in the fridge.

# PESTO

I add fresh pesto to absolutely everything; its nutty, flavourful nature means it tastes wonderful drizzled over vegetables, as a dip for crackers, or as a topping for soups. I've kept this recipe pretty traditional, but you can use a mixture of different herbs instead of the basil for a change.

*makes 250ml or 1 cup*

**10 MINUTES PREPARATION TIME**

50g (½ cup) toasted pine nuts
100g fresh basil leaves
2 large cloves of garlic
½ teaspoon fine sea salt
juice of ½ a lemon
125ml (½ cup) extra virgin olive oil

1. Put all the ingredients except the olive oil into a food processor or blender (either is fine) and whizz until smooth. Add a spoonful of the olive oil, whizz again until incorporated, then keep adding the oil spoonful by spoonful, whizzing after each addition, until it's all used up.

2. Taste, adjust the salt and lemon juice as you want, then either use immediately or transfer to a screwtop jar, cover with a thin layer of olive oil, pop the lid on and store in the fridge for up to a week.

# GUACAMOLE

Fresh guacamole is so easy to make that I feel a bit ashamed calling it a recipe! It's absolutely packed with flavour and is loaded with fresh avocado, coriander, citrus and tomato. Feel free to add the shallot or jalapeño if you like. Serve with vegetable sticks or my seed-sprinkled garlic & oregano crackers (see page 253) as a snack, or add a dollop to meals for a hit of flavour.

*serves 4*

**10 MINUTES PREPARATION TIME**

2 ripe avocados
½ teaspoon fine sea salt
the juice of ½ a lemon or lime
a handful of fresh coriander,
    finely chopped
1 tomato, deseeded and diced

**OPTIONAL:**
½ a fresh jalapeño, deseeded and
    finely chopped
¼ of a shallot, finely chopped

1. To make a smooth guacamole, put all the ingredients into a food processor and whizz until completely smooth. If you'd prefer chunky guacamole, simply mash everything together in a bowl.

2. Guacamole really doesn't keep very well at all, so serve it immediately and enjoy it.

# SEED-SPRINKLED GARLIC & OREGANO CRACKERS

These are brilliant served alongside soups and stews. They're made up of a nutritious, protein-rich variety of nuts and seeds along with spices, so that every bite is not only delicious but good for you as well. Don't worry if a few break in the process – any shards or crumbles are great sprinkled over salads for a little crunch!

— *makes 24 crackers* —

**10 MINUTES PREPARATION TIME**
**35 MINUTES COOKING TIME**

150g (1 cup) hulled sunflower seeds
2 tablespoons ground flaxseed
   or linseed
75g (½ cup) arrowroot or
   tapioca starch
1 teaspoon fine sea salt
1 teaspoon oregano
1 teaspoon garlic powder
1 tablespoon extra virgin olive oil
60ml (¼ cup) boiling water
a variety of seeds, to sprinkle on top
   (I use poppy seeds, sesame seeds
   and pumpkin seeds)

1. Preheat the oven to 160°C/325°F/gas 3.

2. Put the seeds, arrowroot, sea salt, oregano and garlic into a food processor and process for 3 to 4 minutes, until fine and powdery. Add the oil and water, then whizz until a dough is formed.

3. Place the dough on a sheet of parchment paper, then top this with another sheet and roll the dough out between them using a rolling pin. Remove the top sheet, then cut the large rectangle into 24 pieces (no need to separate them). Sprinkle a variety of seeds on top, then place the parchment paper with the crackers on it on a baking tray and pop into the oven. Bake for 35 minutes, until golden.

4. Let cool for at least 15 minutes before enjoying, or let them cool completely and transfer to an airtight container to enjoy later.

# TORTILLA WRAPS

One of the very first recipes I created for this book, these delicious, easy wraps are great for rolling up into tortillas or serving alongside curries. To save time, they can be cooked in bigger batches and frozen in resealable bags until you need them, when you can warm them up in a hot frying pan for a minute or two. You can make them nut-free by using sunflower seed flour (see page 23) too!

*makes 4*

**10 MINUTES PREPARATION TIME**
**24 MINUTES COOKING TIME**

100g (1 cup) ground almonds
150g (1 cup) arrowroot
¾ teaspoon fine sea salt
1 teaspoon of dried herbs of your choice (I love oregano or rosemary!)
80ml (⅓ cup) very hot water
1 tablespoon of olive oil

1. Mix together the ground almonds, arrowroot, salt and herbs in a big bowl. Add the hot water and olive oil, then knead well for a minute or two to form a smooth, pliable dough. If the dough is too sticky, add a little more arrowroot, and if it's too stiff, add a splash more hot water. Divide the dough into four pieces.

2. Lay down a piece of parchment paper, then dust with a little bit of arrowroot. Place a piece of flatbread dough on top, then cover this with another piece of parchment paper. Use a rolling pin to roll the dough out to an approximate 12cm circle.

3. Heat a frying pan over a medium-high heat, then add a small amount of olive oil and use a paper towel to disperse the oil evenly around the pan.

4. Carefully transfer the rolled-out dough to the frying pan and cook for 2 to 3 minutes, until golden brown spots start to appear on the underside of the wrap – you can check this by lifting up a corner of it.

5. Once it's golden on one side, flip the wrap using a spatula. Cook for a further 2 to 3 minutes, until the second side is dotted with golden spots as well, then transfer the wrap to a plate.

5. Repeat the cooking process for the remaining dough to make 4 large wraps in total. Reheat right before serving by warming each wrap up for 10 seconds each side in a hot frying pan, or place the wraps in an airtight container or a resealable bag and keep frozen until you need them – to defrost, warm the wraps up for about a minute on each side in a hot frying pan and use as normal.

# VANILLA BEAN COCONUT WHIPPED CREAM

Rich, fluffy and creamy, this has to be one of my favourite quick treats. It's great spooned over fresh fruit or served with desserts – I love the coconutty touch it adds to everything. Because you need to let the tins of coconut milk separate overnight before you can make this, I suggest you keep a tin or two at the back of the fridge for whipped cream emergencies!

*makes 250ml or 1 cup*

**10 MINUTES PREPARATION TIME**

2 x 400ml tins of full-fat coconut milk, left in the fridge for 12–24 hours
2 tablespoons maple syrup
1 tablespoon vanilla bean powder

1. Remove the tins of coconut milk from the fridge, carefully turn them upside down, and open them with a tin opener. You should see two distinct layers – one clear watery one (this is the coconut water) and one thick white one (this is the coconut cream). Carefully pour the coconut water from both cans into a bowl and put into the fridge to drink or add to a smoothie later.

2. Using a spoon, scoop the thick white coconut cream from the bottom of the tins into a large bowl. Add the maple syrup and the vanilla bean powder, then whip thoroughly with an electric whisk for 4 to 5 minutes, until the coconut cream is light and fluffy. Use immediately.

# DARK CHOCOLATE ROASTED HAZELNUT SPREAD

This has to be one of my favourite recipes in the book, and one of the simplest – there's something about the combination of dark chocolate and hazelnuts that I find absolutely irresistible. Roasting the hazelnuts brings out so much flavour and fills your house with a wonderful aroma, and when you stir the roasted hazelnut butter with rich, silky melted dark chocolate, it forms a seriously delicious spread! Enjoy on a spoon as a treat or dip pieces of fruit into it for an indulgent snack – strawberries and apples are both fantastic.

*makes 250ml or 1 cup*

**20 MINUTES PREPARATION TIME**
**12 MINUTES COOKING TIME**

500g (3 cups) raw blanched whole hazelnuts (blanched just means their brown, bitter skin has been removed)
100g high-quality dark chocolate or dark chocolate chips (see page 24)
½ teaspoon vanilla bean powder

1. Preheat the oven to 180°C/350°F/gas 4. Spread the blanched hazelnuts on a baking sheet in a single layer and roast them for 10 to 12 minutes, until golden and fragrant.

2. Let the hazelnuts cool for about 5 minutes, then transfer to a strong food processor and whizz for about 10 minutes, until completely smooth and runny, scraping down the sides every few minutes.

3. Meanwhile, place the dark chocolate in a heatproof bowl and set over a saucepan of very hot water. Place the saucepan over medium heat until the chocolate has completely melted. Remove it from the pan.

4. Once the hazelnut butter is runny enough to drizzle from a spoon, add the melted chocolate and the vanilla bean powder to the food processor and blend for another 30 seconds or so. Transfer the butter to a screwtop jar or other container, seal and store at room temperature for up to a week.

# DARK CHOCOLATE GANACHE

Smooth, silky and luxuriously chocolatey, this ganache is a chocolate lover's dream! It's very simple, requiring just two ingredients, but makes a luscious topping drizzled over homemade ice cream or spooned on top of a sliced banana. If you're feeling really indulgent, you can also make an incredible hot chocolate by dolloping a spoonful of ganache into a mug and adding hot almond milk – stir well and enjoy!

*makes 250ml or 1 cup*

15 MINUTES PREPARATION TIME

200ml (¾ cup) full-fat tinned
   coconut milk
200g high-quality dark chocolate or
   dark chocolate chips (see page 24)

1.  Place the coconut milk in a small saucepan over a medium heat and warm through until it just starts to simmer – you want to see a few bubbles popping up to the surface, but don't let it boil.

2.  Meanwhile, place the chocolate in a small bowl. Once the coconut milk is simmering lightly, remove it from the heat and pour it over the chocolate. Let the mixture stand for about 2 minutes, then very gently start to stir it. After about a minute of gentle stirring, the mixture will come together and look smooth and glossy.

3.  Either use immediately or transfer it to a jar, pop the lid on and keep it in the fridge for up to a week. To warm it up again, just stand the jar in a saucepan with a couple of centimetres of very hot water, taking care to avoid getting any water in the jar, for about a minute, and stir well before using.

# VANILLA EXTRACT

I use vanilla extract all the time when I'm baking, and this version is free of unwanted extras. It does contain alcohol, so use it when baking, where the alcohol evaporates due to the heat of the oven. If you'd like a vanilla flavour in smoothies or raw desserts, opt for vanilla bean powder instead, as it doesn't contain alcohol, just ground-up vanilla beans.

## makes 250ml or 1 cup

**10 MINUTES PREPARATION TIME**

10 vanilla beans
250ml (1 cup) vodka

1. Using a sharp knife, cut the vanilla beans in half lengthways — this lets more flavour seep into the extract.

2. Pour all the vodka into a screwtop jar, then add the vanilla beans and seal. Let the vanilla extract mature for 6 to 8 weeks in a cool, dark cupboard, shaking gently every few days to mix it up.

3. Once it's matured, you can either strain it to remove the beans and any bits or you can use it as is. The extract will keep sealed in a glass jar for about 2 years.

# SALTED CARAMEL SAUCE

Soft, sweet, buttery salted caramel sauce is definitely an addictive indulgence! The coconut palm sugar adds a very deep, rich caramel flavour, while the coconut milk makes it lusciously creamy. I prefer to use a coarse, flaky salt here, but if you don't have any on hand you can substitute about ⅓ of a teaspoon of fine sea salt instead.

## *makes 375ml or 1 cup*

**10 MINUTES PREPARATION TIME**

60ml (¼ cup) coconut oil
60ml (¼ cup) maple syrup
140g (1 cup) coconut palm sugar
60ml (¼ cup) full-fat tinned
  coconut milk
1 teaspoon vanilla extract
½ teaspoon coarse sea salt

1. Put all the ingredients into a small saucepan over a medium heat. Whisk for 3 to 5 minutes, until the mixture is thick, smooth, and glossy – it might not look like it at first, but you'll get there! Watch out for the mixture foaming up; you need to remove it from the heat as soon as it starts to do this.

2. Use immediately, or, to store, transfer to a screwtop jar and let the sauce cool completely at room temperature before you put on the lid. Keep at room temperature for up to a week.

# THE OTHER BITS
# THAT MAKE UP A
# HEALTHY LIFE

The food you eat isn't the only thing that will help you feel and look better – sleep, stress management, exercise and natural beauty products are all incredibly important and play a huge role in a healthy lifestyle. In fact, I consider them just as important as what I eat!

## STRESS SURVIVAL

Getting plenty of sleep is definitely one of the best ways to combat stress, and, although it might seem a better idea to stay up all night revising for a huge test than making sure you sleep for at least eight hours, it really isn't; many studies have shown that the brain works far, far better when you're not running on a sleep deficit. In the last fifty or so years, the average number of hours we sleep has gone from a solid eight and a half per night to a bleak seven hours — over a whole year, that's the equivalent of losing an entire month of sleep!

Sleep quality is just as important as sleep quantity, though, and there's quite a few things you can do to help this. I know it sounds boring, but staying away from the electronics for at least half an hour before going to bed really improves your circadian rhythm and is an easy thing to try if you're having trouble sleeping well. Read a book or listen to music instead, to help your body and mind wind down after a busy day. Herbal tea can also be very useful with this — my favourites are chamomile, lemon balm and peppermint, or you could try an organic 'sleep' blend.

Being physically active is another huge factor in relieving stress. Aim to move your body for at least half an hour every day. This doesn't have to mean forcing yourself to do something you hate — you could do anything from brisk walking to weight-lifting, running a few miles to dancing — as long as you're being active and building up a sweat. Everybody is different, and it's no use comparing yourself with anybody else because you're an individual, so try to focus on yourself and on doing the things that make you feel great.

# MEDITATION

A quick 5-minute meditation is another one of the easiest ways to get rid of any pent-up stress. You really don't have to be a hermit monk sitting cross-legged in a monastery or a hippie worried about your chakra to meditate, I promise! There are a lot of stereotypes about meditating, and most of them aren't at all true, so give this plan a try to see if it helps you. Remember, though, that you should give it a few tries on different days before you make up your mind; meditation is quite a foreign concept to many of us, so forcing yourself to step back for a few minutes and breathe can take some getting used to!

1. Set a timer for 5 minutes – this way, you won't be worrying about how long you're at it and can focus on your breathing instead. If you can, find a gentle noise to alert you to the end of the 5 minutes rather than a harsh one!

2. Find a comfortable position in a quiet spot. This can be sitting, standing or lying down, with your eyes closed or open – just find what's best for you.

3. Take 10 deep breaths, in through your nose and out through your mouth. Focus on your chest expanding and falling with each breath, pushing away your frustrations and tensions with each breath.

4. Clench then relax your muscles completely from head to toe, beginning with your forehead, your eyes, your jaw, your shoulders and then all the way down to your knees, your feet and your toes. Remember to keep your breathing relaxed while you do this, and try not to let any other thoughts enter your mind.

5. Turn your attention back to your chest rising and falling. Don't try to change the natural pattern or over-think what's happening, but keep focused on the sensation of your breathing. Try to keep this focus for as long as you can. If you notice that your mind has drifted away, don't get annoyed or frustrated but just bring your thoughts back to that rising and falling.

6. When the timer goes, starting at the very tips of your toes and working your way up, clench then relax those muscles again. When you reach your eyes, gently open them if you've had them closed and slowly stand up. You should feel refreshed, relaxed and ready to continue with your day!

YOGA IS ONE OF MY PERSONAL FAVOURITE WAYS TO BEAT STRESS AND BE ACTIVE – HERE ARE A FEW RELAXING SEQUENCES THAT ARE VERY EASY BUT WILL CALM YOU RIGHT DOWN.

## FIRST THING YOGA

When you've woken up late and have a million things running through your head in the morning, I know it sounds silly to spend some of that precious time contorting yourself into all sorts of poses, but doing a bit of yoga in the morning to energize your body is definitely worth setting your alarm 5 minutes earlier for. Remember that you don't have to change into workout clothes and have a yoga mat for this – loose-fitting clothes (hi, pyjamas!) are perfect and there's no equipment needed.

1. **CHILD'S POSE:** I really love this one – it stretches you out and feels great. Kneel on the floor, then take a deep breath and bring your bum over your heels. Stretch your arms forward, then lay your forehead on the floor and relax. Take about 10 deep breaths.

2. **UPWARD FACING DOG:** Lie on the floor with your legs stretched back, your elbows along your sides and your hands beside your waist, then inhale and gently press yourself up to straighten your arms and lift your upper body off the floor. Bring your shoulders back and look up, then take 10 deep breaths.

3. **WARRIOR 1:** Stand up straight, then put one foot in front of you. Turn your back foot about 90 degrees and line the ankle of your back foot up with the back of the front foot. Gently sink down on to your front leg until your knee is right above your ankle. Relax your shoulders down and try to open up your chest, then inhale and bring arms up over your head. Spread out your fingers and relax, then take 5 deep breaths. Repeat on the other side.

4. **CAT-COW POSE:** Begin on your hands and knees, making sure your hips are over your knees and your shoulders directly over your hands. Inhale and arch your back down, lifting your head up as you breathe in. As you exhale, round your back up, pulling your belly button towards the sky. Bring your chin to your chest, then relax your neck. Repeat the cat-cow movement, flowing from the cat movement (back arched and looking up) while you inhale to the cow movement (back curved and looking down) as you exhale for 10 deep breaths.

5. **LOTUS POSE:** Sit cross-legged on the floor and rest your hands on your knees. Roll your shoulders back and try to extend your spine, then take a few deep breaths with your eyes closed and your body relaxed. Repeat with your legs crossed the other way round (with the opposite leg on top). Once you're done, gently stand up and continue with your day, feeling relaxed and refreshed!

1 CHILD'S POSE

2 UPWARD FACING DOG

3 WARRIOR 1

4 CAT-COW POSE

5 LOTUS POSE

**1** SPINAL ROLL POSE

**2** LUNGE TWIST

**5** BRIDGE POSE

**3** FORWARD BEND POSE

**4** CAMEL POSE

# BEFORE BED YOGA

Spending a few minutes doing these gentle, soothing stretches is a great way to wind down after a jam-packed day.

1. **SPINAL ROLL POSE:** Lie down on your back, then bring your knees up to your chest. Wrap your arms around them and gently roll from side to side as you take a few deep breaths, relaxing your spine as you roll.

2. **LUNGE TWIST:** Stand up straight and bring your arms over your head, then put your right foot in front of you and gently lower yourself down until your knee is above your ankle. Place your left hand on the floor, then twist your chest towards your knee to open up. Stretch your right hand up and extend your fingers to really feel the stretch and hold for a few breaths before switching sides and repeating.

3. **FORWARD BEND POSE:** Sit down and cross your legs, then roll your shoulders back and stretch your arms out in front of you. Bend your back forward over your knees and place your extended arms on the floor, gently stretching forwards, hold for a few breaths, then repeat with your legs crossed the other way around (with the opposite leg on top).

4. **CAMEL POSE:** Kneel on the floor with the soles of your feet facing the ceiling, then place your hands on your hips and gently bend backwards, eventually placing your hands on your heels with your arms straight. Arch your back and relax your neck, then take a few deep breaths before very gently bringing yourself up again.

5. **BRIDGE POSE:** Lie down on your back with your arms beside you, the palms of your hands facing down. Bend your knees, then slowly lift your body up. Roll your shoulders back and touch your chin to your chest, then hold for a few breaths before gently returning to lying down.

## LOVING YOUR BODY

I don't mean to be overly cheesy here but I do just want to say how important it is to treat yourself with care, respect, kindness and love. We're bombarded on a daily basis with all sorts of ideals and aspirations of 'perfection' which can make us all feel the need to conform to the unrealistic standards set by the media, and it's so important to shift our mentality and learn how to create a mind full of good thoughts about ourselves.

For every one thing that you don't like about your body, think about and respect all the hundreds of absolutely unbelievable and remarkable things that it does to help you. You can breathe, laugh, think and move – all these things are incredible, and you should encourage yourself to try to appreciate them as much as possible. When you think about all the things your body does, it's hard to not be grateful. Try to focus on thinking about the gift of being healthy and alive rather than being frustrated about the small things, and treat your body with the same kindness and acceptance as you treat your best friend. After all, you wouldn't tell your friend that her hair looks terrible today, so why would you be so critical of yourself?

Replace your negative thoughts with positive ones, right from the moment you wake up. Start each morning with a smile and by thinking about a few things you really like about yourself, and end each evening by thinking of all your wonderful achievements, no matter how small they seem. Next time you look in the mirror, try to be conscious of any negativity, and for every negative thought that comes into your mind, think of two positive ones. You don't have to write them down or say them out loud if you don't want to, but make sure that you think them and, most importantly, believe them!

Rather than comparing yourself with others and putting yourself down, take pride in your individual accomplishments and be happy about them.

Aiming for unrealistic standards or setting yourself conditions like 'I'll only love my body when I can fit into those jeans/run five miles/have more muscle' just fuels unhappiness and negative thoughts, so make sure that you accept the body you have right this moment, just the way it is. That doesn't mean to say you can't be working on your body at the same time, but just ensure that you approach your goals with a love of the body you currently have and make those goals reasonable and attainable. Remember, too, that it's perfectly all right not to be happy with every single part of yourself – nobody is! However, by focusing on the things that you do like, being proud of them and owning them, you're taking a huge step in the right direction. Everyone has bad days, and when they happen, remember to stay positive and think about the things you love about your body rather than the things you want to change.

Lastly, try to spread positivity and support about other peoples' bodies as well. You're not only doing yourself a favour by adopting a more positive mindset, you're also contributing to helping others feel great about themselves. We all struggle with body image, but by complimenting each other instead of constantly judging and criticizing, we can help to form a more supportive society.

I know all that is a lot harder to actually put into practice than it seems, so don't worry if it takes you a while to start appreciating and loving your body! Your size, weight or reflection do not define your worth, your kindness or your personality. You are so much more than that, so love yourself for who you are and remember that a beautiful attitude is most important of all.

## SKIN, HAIR AND BEAUTY

Another enormous part of living a healthier lifestyle is looking at our skin, hair and beauty products. Our skin is our largest organ, so we should be very careful about the things we slather, dab and spray on to it! Many people put at least a few different products on to their skin every single day, and a lot of those can contain harsh chemicals. Luckily, it's easy to make your own skincare and haircare products, which are not only a more natural option but are also often much cheaper than shop-bought alternatives, along with giving great results.

You'll probably be able to find most of the things you need in your kitchen cupboard or at a supermarket – all that's necessary to make yourself a shelf full of natural homemade skin, hair and beauty products are a few ingredients. Try to buy organic oils and waxes wherever possible, raw apple cider vinegar with all its antibacterial properties, and pure essential oils

– I recommend a bottle of tea tree essential oil for face products and another bottle or two of smells you love (jasmine, lemon, ylang ylang, lavender and peppermint are my favourites) to add a delicious scent to your creations. Remember, though, that essential oils are incredibly strong and very concentrated; they should never be used directly on your skin. Be sensible about them – certain essential oils should not be used if you have sensitive skin, are pregnant/breastfeeding or suffer from a medical condition, so do your homework! Stick to the number of drops I've recommended – less is more.

Also, keep in mind that because these homemade mixtures don't contain preservatives, you'll have to be careful that you keep your materials and jars scrupulously clean to avoid any bacteria creeping in. If something starts to look dodgy, toss it!

- *for oily skin:* mix together 2 teaspoons of hazelnut oil and 1 teaspoon of almond oil.

- *for combination skin:* mix together 1 teaspoon each of hazelnut oil and almond oil.

- *for dry skin:* mix together 2 teaspoons of almond oil and 1 teaspoon of hazelnut oil.

Once you've stirred up your oil mix, add a drop of essential oil if you like (I recommend tea tree to help prevent spots), then rinse your face with warm water before gently massaging the oil mix into your skin for about 2 minutes. Grab a clean face towel and run it under water as hot as you can comfortably bear. Lay the hot towel all over your face and press lightly against your skin for about 10 seconds, then gently wipe the oil mixture off your skin. Rinse the towel and repeat if required until your face is completely clean.

2. As a **TONER**, I use a mixture of raw apple cider vinegar and cooled green tea. To make some, pour boiling water into a mug and add a teabag of green tea. Let the tea steep until completely cool, then remove and discard the teabag. Once cool, measure out 125ml (½ cup) of green tea and transfer to a clean jar. Stir 2 tablespoons of raw apple cider vinegar into the green tea and stir well. Add about 5 drops of essential oil (I like tea tree), then seal the jar. To use, simply shake the jar, dip a cotton pad into the mixture and gently apply all over your face after cleansing.

This toner will only last about a week, so toss it when the week is up to prevent bacteria.

3. To **MOISTURIZE**, I'm a complete coconut oil convert! A small dab of coconut oil gently massaged into your face at night will soften you skin beautifully. It might look a tad oily at first, but don't worry – it'll sink in as you sleep.

## FACE

1. To **CLEANSE** your skin, I highly recommend oil cleansing. I know it sounds odd to use oil to cleanse your skin of excess oils, but it really does make sense; the oil you massage into your skin actually helps to dissolve the oil stuck in your pores, so you're essentially gently cleaning out your pores with beneficial, natural oils. By using the right combination, you'll balance your skin's natural oils and leave your skin moisturized and supple. Keep in mind that you will have an adjustment period of a week or two where your skin might look a little worse while your body adapts but after that, you should experience clearer, glowing skin. If you have sensitive skin, it might be a good idea to test a bit of the mixture on the inside of your wrists a few hours before you put any on your face.

4. About once a week, I like to use a fresh face mask to **REJUVENATE** my skin. Making these from natural, fresh ingredients means they're a simple, fun and edible way to pamper yourself.

- *honey and banana mask:* Mash together a banana, a spoonful of honey and a squeeze of lemon juice in a bowl, spread over your skin and leave for 15 minutes before rinsing – the enzymes in raw honey clarify skin while the banana moisturizes and the lemon juice evens skin tone.

- *avocado mask:* Mash a ripe avocado, a spoonful of honey, and a very small splash of apple cider vinegar in a bowl, apply and leave for 15 minutes before rinsing off. Avocado is incredibly rich in omega-3 fatty acids and vitamin C, while the honey boosts hydration and apple cider vinegar has antibacterial properties.

- *cinnamon and honey mask:* Simply stir together a spoonful of honey with a dash of cinnamon and a dash of nutmeg, spread over your face and let it sit for 20 minutes before rinsing. Cinnamon is great for combating spots.

- *strawberry mask:* Mash up a few strawberries with a fork, then apply all over your T-zone. Let it sit for 15 minutes before rinsing off. This is great for balancing out your skin's natural oils.

5. **EXFOLIATING** your skin is also very important. I use a very simple sugar scrub on my arms, legs and lips – simply stir together 140g (1 cup) of raw cane sugar, a few spoonfuls of coconut oil and about 10 drops of your favourite essential oil in a jar to make a thick paste. Gently rub over your skin and rinse off – it's that easy!

**2.** I tend to use either a Faith in Nature **CONDITIONER** or an apple cider vinegar rinse as a conditioner. Apple cider vinegar (it's not as yucky as it sounds, I promise!) adds incredible shine to your hair, and once you've rinsed it out well you won't smell a thing. Mix 2 tablespoons of raw apple cider vinegar with 125ml (½ cup) of warm water, then pour over the ends of clean, wet hair. Take care not to get it in your eyes, as it'll really sting. Rinse out very well a few times and dry your hair as usual.

**3.** A good **DEEP CONDITIONING** with a homemade hair mask is great for making your hair thick, strong and shiny.

- *banana and avocado mask:* *Mash a ripe banana, a ripe avocado and a splash of coconut oil in a small bowl. Wet your hair, then apply the mask and let it sit for 20 minutes before shampooing it out. Apply a small amount of conditioner, rinse out and dry as usual.*

- *coconut oil mask:* *Apply a tablespoon of coconut oil to the ends of dry hair, leave in for half an hour, then shampoo out. Depending on your hair type, you may have to shampoo twice to get the coconut oil out properly. Apply a tiny amount of conditioner if needed, rinse out and dry as usual.*

**4.** **DRY SHAMPOO** is one of the easiest things to make yourself! If your hair is light, simply use a scoopful of arrowroot or tapioca starch. If you have dark hair, use half cacao powder and half arrowroot or tapioca starch and mix with a spoon. Store in small jars. To apply, either use an old make-up brush to lightly dust the mixture on to the roots of your hair, or put it into an old salt or pepper shaker and shake evenly over your roots before rubbing it in and brushing thoroughly.

## HAIR

**1.** I use a herb-infused **SHAMPOO** to strengthen and nurture my hair. Purchase the mildest shampoo you can find – I love the Faith in Nature brand – and make sure that there are no parabens or fragrances in the ingredient list. Choose a herb from the list below and place a handful of it in a large bowl along with 125ml (½ cup) of boiling water. Leave to infuse for about an hour, then remove and discard the herbs, leaving the infused water in the bowl. Add 400ml (about 1½ cups) of shampoo and stir very well to combine. For easier use, I then like to transfer the mixture back to the shampoo bottle.

- *for dry hair:* *chamomile flowers, elderflower, lavender, parsley.*

- *for oily hair:* *rosemary, peppermint, lemongrass, dandelion.*

- *for volume:* *thyme, lavender, sage.*

## LIP BALM AND LOTION

**LIP BALM** couldn't be easier to make, and you can play around with flavours too. Store it in an old clean lip balm pot – or you can purchase empty lip balm tubes online if you like. Put 1 tablespoon of grated beeswax, 2 tablespoons of cacao butter and 1 tablespoon of almond oil into a small saucepan and set over a low heat until completely melted. Remove from the heat and stir in about 5 drops of essential oil of choice (I like peppermint). Either divide the mixture between two or three old pots, or carefully divide it between a few lip balm tubes, and let it sit for about an hour, until set. The lip balm will stay good for about a year.

My recipe for **BODY LOTION** is a little more advanced, so it's great if you want to try something slightly trickier! (Simply using pure coconut oil on its own is a good option as well.)

To make the lotion, place 250ml (1 cup) of hazelnut or almond oil and 30g of natural beeswax pellets in a heatproof bowl and set the bowl over a saucepan filled about a quarter of the way up with hot water. Melt over a low heat, stirring occasionally, until completely melted. Let the mixture cool at room temperature for up to an hour, until it has almost solidified, then add up to 8 drops of an essential oil of your choice and use a hand-held blender to whisk until fluffy and light. You only need a very small amount, and it's best to apply it before bed as it needs some time to sink in. Transfer to a clean glass jar and store at room temperature for up to 3 months.

## TOOTHPASTE AND DEODORANT

Most **TOOTHPASTES** contain all sorts of artificial flavours, colours and additives. This easy homemade toothpaste uses coconut oil and bicarbonate of soda to clean and nourish teeth – just use a hand-held blender to whip together 125ml (½ cup) of coconut oil and 140g (½ cup) of bicarbonate of soda along with 10 drops of peppermint essential oil. Store in a jar and use like normal toothpaste – if it's warm, it might melt a little and you may have to give it a good stir to mix it all up before using.

The harsh and toxic chemicals in shop-bought **DEODORANTS** and antiperspirants are definitely something you'll want to avoid – this homemade deodorant is an effective and natural solution. Keep in mind that you might have an adjustment period of a few days where you need to apply it twice or three times a day, but after that applying it once a day onto clean, dry armpits will suffice. Also remember that this is a deodorant rather than an antiperspirant, so while it'll stop the stink you might still sweat a little, which is perfectly natural.

To make it, combine 35g (¼ cup) of arrowroot, 35g (¼ cup) of bicarbonate of soda and 60ml (¼ cup) of coconut oil in a small container to make a thick paste. Store in a sealed container in a cool, dry place – if it's warm, it may melt and you'll have to give it a good stir before use. To use, apply just a little bit to each armpit and gently rub in. If you have particularly sensitive skin, you may experience redness or a rash after use – if so, make another batch but use 70g (½ cup) of arrowroot and leave out the bicarbonate of soda.

# INDEX

goji berries: pomegranate, orange and goji berry mince pies 221
granita: watermelon, lime and mint granita 184
granola: date and almond granola bars 58
  pecan, coconut and lemon granola 51
green beans: garlicky green beans with cherry tomatoes and balsamic 102
green smoothie 46
guacamole 250

hair products 276, 280
hazelnuts: chocolate hazelnut freezer fudge 192
  chocolate and hazelnut truffles 195
  dark chocolate roasted hazelnut spread 259
  hazelnut butter 40
  hazelnut cacao energy bars 178
  hazelnut chocolate chip waffles 72
herbs 19
  see also individual herbs
honey 23
  cinnamon and honey face mask 279
  honey and banana face mask 279
  honey sesame chicken with baby bok choy 144

ice cream: chocolate-dipped almond ice cream bars 234
  salted caramel coconut ice cream parfaits 216
  summer berry crumble with chai coconut ice cream 233
ice lollies: chocolate coconut ice lollies 222
  rainbow coconut water ice lollies 227

jam: raspberry chia jam 66

kitchen equipment 26–27
kiwis: rainbow coconut water ice lollies 227
knife skills 29

lemons: almond and lemon-crusted wild salmon 128
  cucumber-lemon-blueberry water 244
  lemon-garlic chicken marinade 39
  lemon garlic vinaigrette 247
  lemon poppyseed scones 66
  lemon zest, blueberry and almond French madeleines 239
  pecan, coconut and lemon granola 51
  pesto scrambled eggs with avocado and garlic-lemon spinach 54

lettuce: apricot and mint chicken romaine boats 116
limes: mango lime tart 228
  pomegranate, lime and raspberry spritzers 170
  sweet potato vegetable pad Thai with lime, tahini and ginger dressing 122
  watermelon, lime and mint granita 184
lip balm 283

macaroons: raw cacao coconut macaroons 204
madeleines: lemon zest, blueberry and almond French madeleines 239
mangoes: mango lime tart 228
  pineapple-pomegranate-mango water 244
  rainbow coconut water ice lollies 227
maple syrup 24
  cinnamon maple glazed walnuts 201
  maple meringues with coconut, berries and passionfruit 162
  toasted maple cinnamon coconut chips 183
marinades 39
meal planning and preparing 32–33
meat 15–16, 38–39
  see also individual meats
meatballs in Moroccan tomato sauce 136
meditation 268
meringues: maple meringues with coconut, berries and passionfruit 162
Mexican burgers with all the toppings 130
mince pies: pomegranate, orange and goji berry mince pies 221
mint: apricot and mint chicken romaine boats 116
  orange-strawberry-mint water 244
  tomato, mint and parsley chopped salad 98
  watermelon, lime and mint granita 184
muffins: carrot, coconut and pineapple muffins 57
mushrooms: egg, bacon, mushroom and chive cups 64
  parsley and chive pesto stuffed mushrooms 161
  sautéed mushrooms with garlic and parsley 107
mustard and dill sauce 39

nuts 15, 22
  homemade nut butters and nut milks 40
  nut and date energy bites 198

see also individual nuts

oils 15
  for face 278
  see also coconut oil
omegas 19
onions: cucumber red onion salad 101
  see also shallots; spring onions
oranges: fancy fruit salad 230
  orange vinaigrette 247
  orange-ginger beef, broccoli and bok choy stir-fry 118
  orange-strawberry-mint water 244
  overnight banana orange chia pudding 63
  pomegranate, orange and goji berry mince pies 221
oregano: mini flaxseed and oregano pizzas 164
  seed-sprinkled garlic and oregano crackers 253

pad Thai: sweet potato vegetable pad Thai 122
pancakes 70
paprika and cayenne beef rub 39
parsley: parsley and chive pesto stuffed mushrooms 161
  sautéed mushrooms with garlic and parsley 107
  tomato, mint and parsley chopped salad 98
passionfruit: fancy fruit salad 230
  maple meringues with coconut, berries and passionfruit 162
  pineapple carrot cake with passionfruit coconut frosting 224
peaches: cinnamon stewed peaches with pecan crunch 215
peas: cucumber ribbon, radish, spring onion and sugar snap salad 95
  pea and pepper beef curry 148
pecans: cinnamon stewed peaches with pecan crunch 215
  crunchy nut banana loaf 189
  fudgy raspberry chocolate tartlets with cacao and toasted pecan crust 152
  pecan, coconut and lemon granola 51
peppers: breakfast burrito wraps 69
  easy roasted veg 110
  pea and pepper beef curry 148
  red pepper chicken fajitas 127
  roasted pollack with red pepper, tomatoes and chilli 133–34
  spicy Thai red curry soup 89
pesto 248
  parsley and chive pesto stuffed mushrooms 161
  pesto scrambled eggs 54

# WITH THANKS TO

There is absolutely no way that I would be where I am today without the help and support of many lovely people, and I'd like to say a massive thanks to everyone who has helped along the way!

Thank you to my family for their endless support, washing-up and supermarket trips; to my mum, thank you for teaching me the fun in cooking, to my dad, thank you for your advice and encouragement, and to my brother Tim, for all of your tech support and your willingness to eat all the leftovers! My grandparents and extended family deserve a very special mention too.

Enormous thanks to my lovely editor Lindsey Evans and the fabulous Zoë Berville for all your encouragement and your belief in me right from the very first email. I would never have been able to do it without your help and guidance!

Massive thanks to all of the lovely people at Penguin for turning my crazy ideas into a real-life book and making it such a wonderful experience: Nikki Dupin, Annie Lee, Anjali Nathani, Catherine Wood, Aimie Price, Beatrix McIntyre, Katya Shipster, Hattie Adam-Smith, and Isabel Coburn and the sales team.

Huge thanks to Stephanie Susinski for your support, advice, encouragement and texts. I'm so incredibly lucky to have a friend like you!

To Issy Croker, for capturing the essence of this book so perfectly with your stunning lifestyle photography.

Thank you to the friends who have shared all of my excitement on this crazy journey – Alexia, Paula, Nikki, Emma, Ceres, Lorena, Lucy, Laura and of course Anthea and Elizan!

To the brands who have let me experiment with their fantastic products for this book – Biona, Lakeland, Magimix and Real Food Source.

Big thanks to Lembas Organics farm in Aberdeenshire for welcoming us to your beautiful

farm and letting us take pictures of adorable ducklings, beautiful greens and stunning scenery!

To Ilana McGrath and Matt Errico, my old English teachers, for showing me the power of words and inspiring me to start blogging and writing.

Lastly, thank you to everyone who has followed my blog, read my posts and bought this book – I truly hope you love it and I can't thank you enough for your support. I owe you all a big hug and a cookie!